Food Retailing Mathematics
A Practical Approach

Food Retailing Mathematics
A Practical Approach

Daniel J. McLaughlin, Jr.

Chain Store Age Books

An Affiliate of Lebhar-Friedman, Inc.
New York

Library of Congress Cataloging in Publication Data

McLaughlin, Daniel J
  Food retailing mathematics.

  Includes bibliographical references.
  1. Business mathematics—Food industry and trade. I. Title.
HF5695.5.F616M32   513′.93   75-11696
ISBN 0-912016 40-X

Dedication

In memory of my late father, who loved
both books and numbers; this seems
somehow appropriate.

Preface

This book is designed for all of us who have great difficulty with arithmetic and mathematics. The purpose is to apply these basic techniques as simply and as painlessly as possible to the management of the modern food market.

As in any book, many people worked on the project, but there are a few people who deserve special thanks: James Toothman, formerly with Saint Joseph's and now at the Pennsylvania State University, who always insisted there was a need for this type of analysis; Charles Mallowe, the Associate Administrator of the Academy of Food Marketing, who has struggled for years teaching a course in this area; and Kathleen McGinty, St. Joseph's Class of 1975, who did the really hard work of editing the manuscript.

Daniel J. McLaughlin, Jr.
Center Square, Pennsylvania

Contents

Preface   vii

Part I: The Basics   1

   1   Arithmetic in the Food Store   3

   2   Basic Arithmetic Review   7

Part II: Basic Measurement and Relationships   21

   3   Fractions   23

   4   The Decimal System   35

   5   The Metric System   45

   6   Simple Relationships   57

Part III: Food Store Operating Problems   67

   7   Operating Statements and Gross Margin   69

 8   Markups and Margins   79

 9   Inventory Control and Turnover   89

10   Discounts and Discounting   97

11   Unit Pricing and Other Consumer Aids   107

12   Payroll and Work Scheduling   121

13   Operating Ratios   131

14   Retail Food Store Operating Problems   147

Appendix   167

Glossary   175

The Author   181

Part I

The Basics

In this first brief section, we are concerned with the importance of arithmetic and a review of the basic operations required to solve problems. Even though the reader obviously knows basic mathematical operations, it is well to spend a few moments on the following two chapters as a refresher course in these simple concepts.

A short time spent on this section now will make the succeeding chapters much more relevant.

1

Arithmetic in the Food Store

The food store is a world of numbers. The store operator, manager, and employees are all surrounded by that world—daily confronted with prices, weights, sizes, quantities, volumes, costs, expenses, payrolls, receipts, bills, invoices, computer print-outs, and hundreds of other details involving numbers. The ability of store people to perform basic mathematical operations is more critical today than ever before because the modern food store is changing in many ways. The following factors have contributed to these changes:

- Inflation, shortages of many items, and the energy crunch have brought about increases in food prices, with the result that consumers are increasingly price- and quality-conscious.
- The cost of owning and operating a food store has increased dramatically.
- Labor costs are rising and will continue to rise as inflation eats into workers' salaries.

- The number of manufactured food products continues to increase at a time when many food stores are trying to decrease the number of items they stock.

- Supermarkets are carrying more and more non-food items, which demand new mathematical ratios and relationships in food store accounting.

- Discounting and price warfare cause frequent price changes and cut margins to record lows.

- Since net earnings as a percent of sales in most food stores have been cut to less than one percent, there is very little room for mistake or miscalculation on the part of store employees.

- The increasing use of computers for such activities as ordering, inventory control, price changes, etc. makes it necessary for store people to understand basic computer symbols and print-outs. The Universal Product Code (UPC) has already been adopted by major food retailing chains and may *reduce* the demands made for competence in some arithmetic computations.

- Metric weights (SI or International System of Units) are beginning to appear on more and more canned and packaged foods. The metric system, described in Chapter 5, is already used by most countries in the world. Very shortly, the United States Congress is expected to require our adoption of the metric system through a series of steps that would be completed within a 10-year period. Food stores and the people who operate and work in them will undoubtedly be among the first to feel the effect of this change. Even without an official Congressional law, however, metrification is becoming more accepted in the U.S. In many states, road signs, altitude markers, and other signs are being marked in both conventional and metric measurements. Many industries are making use of testing equipment which is becoming available with metric gradations so that testing to metric standards can now be accomplished. In packaging, such items as cigarette packs and wine bottles are being marked with metric measurements.[1]

The tremendous pressure from these and many other factors has changed the nature of food store operations. Store managers and department heads should be responsible primarily for the marketing and merchandising of food and related products, but factors like those listed above often leave them too little time for the performance of their primary functions. The manipulation of numbers is just one of many time-consuming annoyances; however, it is an area where improvement is possible. This book is concerned with simple arithmetic and how it can be applied to store operations. It is hoped that these few techniques will help food store employees in their vital work of marketing and distributing food.

---

[1] *Research Institute Recommendations,* October 25, 1974, The Research Institute of America.

2

Basic Arithmetic Review

This chapter covers the four basic operations in arithmetic—addition, subtraction, multiplication, and division—and is designed as a refresher course in these simple calculations. Even the most experienced food store managers and employees will admit that under the pressure of the typical working day, they occasionally will "black out" and forget how to perform the easiest types of calculations.

The problems in this chapter are in pure numbers. They are for arithmetic exercise purposes only. The problems in the remaining chapters will be related to actual food store problems.

Work out these problems by yourself, using pencil and paper (no pocket calculators!) Time yourself in order to test both speed and accuracy. (Calculators may be used only to check your work and results.)

2-1 ADDITION

Addition is the process of combining two or more numbers to obtain a single quantity or result. It is, of course, the basic operation of all cash registers and checkout systems.

Examples:

	1.	720	2.	3,145	3.	17
		+ 180		+ 225		8
		900		3,370		9
						22
						+ 27
						83

Problems 2–1

(These problems should take approximately four minutes to complete.)

(1)
```
      89
    + 17
```

(2)
```
     312
   + 608
```

(3)
```
    4,117
  + 5,117
```

(4)
```
    6,400
  +    17
```

(5)
```
   10,712
    9,168
  + 4,222
```

(6)
```
      727
      709
       16
       35
    1,112
  +   437
```

(7)
```
    1,422
      636
    1,712
    1,896
        4
  +    73
```

(8)
```
  100,116
   87,212
  +  3,116
```

(9)
```
   12,113
    9,116
   13,792
  +  4,712
```

(10)
```
       72
       16
        8
        9
  +    12
```

2–2 SUBTRACTION

Subtraction is the process of finding the difference between numbers. It is especially important in making correct change for customers.

Examples: 1.   916   2.   12,313   3. $20.00
                     − 312   − 4,701   − 17.27
                    ―――――   ――――――   ―――――――
                      604   7,612 $ 2.73

Problems 2–2

(These problems should take approximately six minutes to complete.)

(1)   96   (6)   12,617
             − 35   −   87
           ――――――   ――――――――

(2)   351   (7)   2,000,004
            − 176   − 179,210
           ――――――   ――――――――

(3)   4,879   (8)   996
          − 3,202   − 199
           ――――――   ――――――――

(4)   19,912   (9)   779
        − 13,670   − 776
           ――――――   ――――――――

(5)   237,676   (10)   212,432
        − 189,212   − 199,999
           ――――――   ――――――――

2–3 MULTIPLICATION

Multiplication is the process of combining one number as many times as there are units in another number; this results in a product. The prices of all meat items and most produce items are arrived at by multiplying the weight by the unit price.

Examples: 1.   84   2.   96
                           × 7   × 23
                          ――――――   ――――――
                            588   288
                                               192
                                             ――――――
                                              2208

3. $ 1.99 per lb.
      ×   2 lbs.
      $ 3.98 total price

Problems 2–3

(These problems should take approximately eight minutes to complete.)

(1)   13   (6)   2,718
       × 9   × 97

(2)   27   (7)   414
       × 6   × 84

(3)   39   (8)   7,412
       × 13   × 360

(4)   314   (9)   9,672
       × 72   × 3,809

(5) 5,000   (10)   717
       × 25   × 89

2–4 DIVISION

Division, the process of finding how many times one number is contained in another, results in a quotient. All unit price concepts are based on dividing the total price by the weight to arrive at some comparable unit price. The dividend is the number being divided. The divisor is the number by which it is being divided.

Examples: 39   28   17
                      1. 8/312   2. 20/560   3. 22/374
                           24   40   22
                           72   160   154
                           72   160   154

Problems 2–4

(These problems should take approximately 10 minutes to complete.)

(1) 6/24̅

(2) 9/63̅

(3) 25/425̅

(4) 18/324̅

(5) 60/12,000̅

(6) 72/936̅

(7) 33/1,012̅

(8) 200/386,000̅

(9) 12/111̅

(10) 18/1,620̅

These four arithmetic forms are the basis of all the problems to be discussed in this book. An understanding of these basics is vital to the understanding of the succeeding sections.

ANSWERS

2–1

(1)	106	(6)	3,036
(2)	920	(7)	5,743
(3)	9,234	(8)	190,444
(4)	6,417	(9)	39,733
(5)	24,102	(10)	117

2–2

(1)	61	(6)	12,530
(2)	175	(7)	1,820,794
(3)	1,677	(8)	797
(4)	6,242	(9)	3
(5)	48,464	(10)	12,433

2–3

(1)	117	(6)	263,646
(2)	162	(7)	34,776
(3)	507	(8)	2,668,320
(4)	22,608	(9)	36,840,648
(5)	125,000	(10)	63,813

2–4

(1)	4	(6)	13
(2)	7	(7)	30.67
(3)	17	(8)	1,930
(4)	18	(9)	9.25
(5)	200	(10)	90

Work Space

Work Space

Work Space

Work Space

Work Space

Work Space

Work Space

Work Space

Part II

Basic Measurement and Relationships

This is the "how-to" section of food store arithmetic. In some detail, the following chapters cover fractions, decimals, ratios, proportions, and percentages. We also will discuss the metric system of measurement.

The subjects of the chapters in Part II are closely interrelated and are isolated here for study purposes only. Part III brings the techniques reviewed in Part II into focus to be used to solve real operating problems in a food store.

3

Fractions

Fractions are less commonly used than decimals and may decline in importance even more with a future conversion to the metric system (see Chapter 5). However, they are still a useful and necessary part of arithmetic.

A fraction is a part or a portion of the totality of something. The numerator expresses the number of parts that have been taken from the whole. The denominator is the number of parts into which the total has been divided.

Example:

$$\frac{3}{4} \quad \begin{array}{l} \text{Numerator} \\ \hline \text{Denominator} \end{array}$$

A pound of ground sirloin is divided into eight equal patties. If one patty is broiled and eaten, the remainder is expressed as a fractional part:

$$\text{Remainder} = \frac{7}{8}$$

7=the numerator, or number of equal patties left of the whole.

8=the denominator, or the number of equal patties into which the pound of sirloin was originally divided.

Proper fractions are those in which the numerator is less than the denominator; and improper fractions are those which have a numerator equal to or greater than the denominator.

Proper Fractions: $\dfrac{3}{4}$ $\dfrac{7}{8}$ $\dfrac{1}{3}$ $\dfrac{15}{16}$

Improper Fractions: $\dfrac{4}{3}\left(=1\tfrac{1}{3}\right)\dfrac{8}{7}\left(=1\tfrac{1}{7}\right)\dfrac{8}{5}\left(=1\tfrac{3}{5}\right)\dfrac{4}{4}\left(=1\right)$

There are a few other simple operations that make fractions easier to manipulate arithmetically. Fractions are often *reduced* to make them simpler to work with. Reduction simply means avoiding larger numbers in favor of smaller numbers, which are easier to handle.

Examples: 1. $\dfrac{8}{24}=\dfrac{1}{3}$, divide 24 by 8 to reduce to $\dfrac{1}{3}$

2. $\dfrac{6}{24}=\dfrac{1}{4}$, divide 24 by 6 to reduce to $\dfrac{1}{4}$

The use of a *common denominator* aids in the solution of many fractional problems. The common denominator is a larger number into which all the denominators in the problem can be proportionately combined. It is most often used in addition and subtraction.

Examples: 1.   For $\dfrac{1}{3}$, $\dfrac{3}{4}$, $\dfrac{5}{6}$, $\dfrac{7}{8}$, the common denominator is 24 because 3, 4, 6, and 8 all fit into 24 evenly.

2. For $\dfrac{4}{5}$, $\dfrac{5}{6}$, $\dfrac{3}{10}$, $\dfrac{2}{15}$, the common denominator is 30.

3. $\dfrac{24}{36} = \dfrac{2}{3}$, divide 24 and 30 by a common denominator (12) to reduce to $\dfrac{2}{3}$

4. $\dfrac{48}{36} = \dfrac{4}{3}$, divide 48 and 36 by a common denominator (12) to reduce to $\dfrac{4}{3}$

The division of fractions (see section 3–4) is greatly simplified by the use of a *reciprocal*. A reciprocal is really the quotient of one unit, divided by any quantity. For purposes of this chapter, a reciprocal is found by inverting a fraction or simply turning it upside-down.

Examples:

1. $\dfrac{2}{3}$ becomes $\dfrac{3}{2}$

2. $\dfrac{7}{8}$ becomes $\dfrac{8}{7}$

The four basic arithmetic operations can be used on fractions as explained in the following sections.

3–1 ADDITION

In order to add fractions, the denominators must first be reduced to a common number, called the lowest common denominator (see above). After this is done, the numerators are simply added together.

Examples:

1. Add $\dfrac{2}{5}, \dfrac{3}{5}, \dfrac{4}{5}, \dfrac{1}{5}, = \dfrac{2+3+4+1}{5}$

$= \dfrac{10}{5} = 2$

2. Add $\dfrac{4}{6}, \dfrac{2}{8}, \dfrac{3}{12}, \dfrac{3}{4}$; the common denominator is 24. Thus, the fractions become $\dfrac{16}{24}, \dfrac{6}{24}, \dfrac{6}{24}, \dfrac{18}{24} = \dfrac{46}{24}$

$= 1\dfrac{22}{24} = 1\dfrac{11}{12}$

Problems 3–1

Add:

(1) $\dfrac{3}{9}, \dfrac{4}{9}, \dfrac{1}{9}, \dfrac{8}{9}$

(2) $\dfrac{3}{9}, \dfrac{4}{6}, \dfrac{3}{12}, \dfrac{2}{18}$

(3) $\dfrac{2}{5}, \dfrac{4}{7}, \dfrac{4}{5}, \dfrac{6}{7}$

(4) $\dfrac{4}{5}, \dfrac{5}{6}, \dfrac{7}{10}, \dfrac{8}{3}$

(5) $\dfrac{4}{8}, \dfrac{5}{6}, \dfrac{2}{3}, \dfrac{3}{4}$

3–2 SUBTRACTION

In order to subtract fractions, find a common denominator as in addition, and then simply subtract the numerators.

Examples:

1. Subtract $\dfrac{1}{4}$ from $\dfrac{3}{4} = \dfrac{2}{4} = \dfrac{1}{2} = .50$ (in decimals)[1]

---

[1] To get the decimal, divide denominator into numerator: $2\,\overline{\smash{)}\,1.00}$ → $.50$

2. Subtract $\frac{1}{2}$ from $\frac{7}{8}$

common denominator is 16

$\frac{8}{16}$ from $\frac{14}{16} = \frac{6}{16} = \frac{3}{8} = .375$ (in decimals)

Problems 3–2

Subtract:

(1) $\frac{9}{16}$ from $\frac{13}{16}$

(2) $\frac{5}{6}$ from $\frac{6}{7}$

(3) $\frac{3}{4}$ from $\frac{7}{8}$

(4) $\frac{6}{4}$ from $\frac{5}{3}$

(5) $\frac{5}{6}$ from $\frac{8}{9}$

3–3 MULTIPLICATION

To multiply fractions, find the products of the numerators and denominators.

Examples:

1. Multiply $\frac{4}{12} \times \frac{3}{9} = \frac{12}{108} = \frac{1}{9} = .11$ (in decimals)

2. Multiply $\frac{5}{4} \times \frac{4}{16} = \frac{20}{64} = \frac{5}{16} = .31$ (in decimals)

Problems 3–3

Multiply:

(1) $\frac{5}{6} \times \frac{7}{8}$

(2) $\dfrac{9}{16} \times \dfrac{3}{24}$

(3) $\dfrac{4}{12} \times \dfrac{3}{16}$

(4) $\dfrac{3}{5} \times \dfrac{6}{7}$

(5) $\dfrac{2}{3} \times \dfrac{4}{9}$

3–4 DIVISION

The division of fractions is slightly more difficult because a *reciprocal* is commonly used. The reciprocal is found by inverting the divisor. Then, the fractions are multiplied.

Example: Divide $\dfrac{3}{5} \div \dfrac{2}{3} =$

$\dfrac{3}{5} \times \dfrac{3}{2}$ (inverted divisor or recipro-

cal) $= \dfrac{9}{10} = .90$ (in decimals)

Problems 3–4

Divide:

(1) $\dfrac{7}{16} \div \dfrac{2}{3}$

(2) $\dfrac{3}{27} \div \dfrac{4}{5}$

(3) $\dfrac{2}{7} \div \dfrac{3}{4}$

(4) $\dfrac{2}{5} \div \dfrac{3}{4}$

(5) $\dfrac{2}{7} \div \dfrac{5}{6}$

ANSWERS

3–1

(1) $\dfrac{16}{9} = 1.77$

(2) Common Denominator $36 = \dfrac{49}{36} = 1.36$

(3) Common Denominator $35 = \dfrac{92}{35} = 2.63$

(4) Common Denominator $30 = \dfrac{150}{30} = 5$

(5) Common Denominator $24 = \dfrac{66}{24} = 2.75$

3–2

(1) $\dfrac{4}{16} = \dfrac{1}{4} = .25$

(2) Common Denominator $42 = \dfrac{1}{42} = .02$

(3) Common Denominator $8 = \dfrac{1}{8} = .125$

(4) Common Denominator $12 = \dfrac{1}{6} = .166$

(5) Common Denominator $18 = \dfrac{1}{18} = .055$

3–3

(1) $\dfrac{35}{48} = .73$

(2) $\dfrac{27}{384} = .07$

(3) $\dfrac{12}{192} = .06$

(4) $\dfrac{18}{35} = .51$

(5) $\dfrac{6}{27} = .22$

3–4

(1) $\dfrac{7}{16} \times \dfrac{3}{2} = \dfrac{21}{32} = .66$

(2) $\dfrac{3}{27} \times \dfrac{5}{4} = \dfrac{15}{108} = .14$

(3) $\dfrac{2}{7} \times \dfrac{4}{3} = \dfrac{8}{21} = .38$

(4) $\dfrac{2}{5} \times \dfrac{4}{3} = \dfrac{8}{15} = .53$

(5) $\dfrac{2}{7} \times \dfrac{6}{5} = \dfrac{12}{35} = .34$

Work Space

Work Space

Work Space

Work Space

4

The Decimal System

The decimal system is designed to separate whole numbers and decimal fractions. Currently, decimals are more widely used than fractions in normal store operations; when the U.S. converts to the metric system (see Chapter 5), decimals will become even more important.

The decimal system is a system of notation thought to have been developed in India and passed by the Arab peoples to Europeans sometime in the early Middle Ages. It is far more convenient to use than the fractional system. The American monetary system always has been based on decimals. However, our measurement system is based on the British system which usually results in the more difficult-to-handle fractional measures.

The decimal point or dot (.) is used as a separation point. The numbers to the left of the decimal point indicate units, tens, hundreds, thousands, tens of thousands, etc. The numbers to the right of the decimal point indicate tenths, hundredths, thousandths, etc.

Example:

units   0.0   tenths
tens   00.00   hundredths
hundreds   000.000   thousandths
thousands   0000.0000   ten thousandths
tens of thousands   00 000.00000   hundred thousandths
hundred thousands   000 000.00000
millions   0 000 000.00000

The four basic arithmetic operations may be performed on decimals.

4–1 ADDITION AND SUBTRACTION

To add and subtract numbers with decimals, simply place decimals of corresponding power in the same vertical column; and then perform the normal operation.

Examples:

1.
$$
\begin{array}{r}
126.2 \\
4.72 \\
+\ \ 87.3 \\
\hline
218.22
\end{array}
$$

2.
$$
\begin{array}{r}
10,387.6 \\
512.9 \\
+\ \ \ \ \ 6.9 \\
\hline
10,907.4
\end{array}
$$

3.
$$
\begin{array}{r}
427.63 \\
-\ 317.27 \\
\hline
110.36
\end{array}
$$

4.
$$
\begin{array}{r}
94.16 \\
-\ 89.93 \\
\hline
4.23
\end{array}
$$

Problems 4–1

(1)   4.6
       2.3
       7.2

(2)   18.23
     12.24
     19.07

(3) 437.2
     62.93
      2.0

(4) 7,327.6
   1,444.4
     72.3

(5)   9.17
      2.30
      4.96
    12.18

(6) 137.49
  −   8.21

(7)   16.1
  − 4.9

(8) 10,327.63
  − 9,991.18

(9) 163.00
  − 97.99

(10) 404.08
   − 20.98

(11)   6.4
     5.3
     9.2

(12) 302.78
  − 165.92

4–2 MULTIPLICATION

When multiplying decimals, the final product will have as many places to the right of the decimal point as there are in the two numbers being multiplied.

Examples:

1.   93.27   2 places
         4.18   2 places
   389.8686   4 places

2.   6.14   2 places
        2.2   1 place
    13.508   3 places

Problems 4–2

Multiply:

(1)   83.7
          2.17
    _____

(2)   9.40
          2.20
    _____

(3)   317.6
          2.391
    _____

(4)   7.3
          2.0
    _____

(5)   87.9
         16.2
    _____

(6)   42.1
          6.3
    _____

(7)   4.11
          .21
    _____

4–3 DIVISION

When dividing with decimals, there should be no decimal point in the divisor. Therefore, the decimal is moved the corresponding number of places in both the dividend and divisor as shown below. (See Chapter 2 for explanation of dividend and divisor.)

Example: .15/830.72   shift to

$$\overline{5538.13}$$
$$\overline{15/83072.00} = \overline{15/83072.00}$$

Problems 4–3

Divide:

(1) $2.8/\overline{18}$

(2) $4.6/\overline{204}$

(3) $20.2/\overline{200}$

(4) $2.28/\overline{4.96}$

(5) $9/\overline{72}$

(6) $3.2/\overline{18.6}$

(7) $2.34/\overline{10.25}$

ANSWERS

4–1

(1)	14.1	(7)	11.2
(2)	49.54	(8)	336.45
(3)	502.13	(9)	65.01
(4)	8,844.3	(10)	383.10
(5)	28.61	(11)	20.9
(6)	129.28	(12)	136.86

4–2

(1)	181.629
(2)	20.6800
(3)	759.3816
(4)	14.60
(5)	1,423.98
(6)	265.23
(7)	.8631

4–3

(1)	6.429
(2)	44.348
(3)	9.90
(4)	2.175
(5)	8
(6)	5.8125
(7)	4.38

Work Space

Work Space

Work Space

Work Space

5

The Metric System

The International System of Units (SI) is the modernized version of the metric system, established by international agreement. It provides a logical and interconnected framework for all measurements in science, industry, and commerce.

The United States is the only major industrialized nation in the world that has not completely adopted the metric system. However, in 1971, Congress created the Metric Conversion Board which is responsible for changing the U.S. over to the metric system, possibly within the next decade. These changes will have significant implications for the entire food industry, and especially for food retailers.

The metric system is actually an easier form of calculating since all measures are in decimals rather than fractions. Americans will have difficulty with it at first only because the system is unfamiliar, not because it is inherently difficult.

There are seven base units of measurement in the metric system. (See Appendix for full metric conversion tables and symbols):

- Length: Meter, m
- Mass: Kilogram, kg
- Time: Second, S
- Electric Current: Ampere, A
- Temperature: Kelvin, K
- Amount of Substance: Mole, Mol
- Luminous Intensity: Candela, cd

Although most Americans do not realize it, the U.S. has already partially adopted the metric system. We use the international measures for time, electric current, amount of substance, and luminous intensity. A full conversion to the metric system would mean that we also would use metric standards for length, mass, and temperature—areas of great concern to food retailers.

5–1 LENGTH AND AREA

The meter is the standard measure of length and is defined as "1,650,763.73 wavelengths in vacuum of the orange-red line of the spectrum of krypton-86." In layman's terms, this is a little more than one yard in length.

These are the standard conversion measures to the metric system for length and area:

Symbol	U.S. System	Multiply by	To Get	Metric System	Symbol
yd.^{3}	inches	25.4		millimeters	mm
in.	feet	30		centimeters	cm
ft.	yards	0.9		meters	m
yd.	miles	1.6		kilometers	km
mi.	square inches	6.5		square centimeters	cm^2
in.^{2}	square feet	0.09		square meters	m^2
ft.^{2}	square yards	0.8		square meters	m^2
yd.^{2}	square miles	2.6		square kilometers	km^2
mi.^{2}	acres	0.4		hectares	ha
	cubic yard	0.76		cubic meters	m^3

Examples: 1.   A supermarket has 20,000 square feet. Convert measurement to metric system.
20,000 sq. ft. × .09 = 1,800 square meters

2.   A frozen food section has 50 linear feet of shelf space. Convert to metric system.
50 ft. × 30 = 1,500 centimeters

Problem 5–1

Supermarket Q is 32,000 square feet, with 27,000 square feet of selling space. The grocery department takes up 16,000 square feet, with 3,000 for meat and 2,500 for produce. Convert size measurements of Store Q to the metric system.

5–2   MASS (WEIGHT)

The kilogram (kg) is the standard measure of mass or weight and is defined by "a cylinder of platinum-iridium alloy kept by the International Bureau of Weights and Measures in Paris." The only base measure still defined by an artifact rather than a scientific measure, the kilogram is slightly more than two pounds.

These are the conversion measures to the metric system for weight and volume:

Symbol	U.S. System	Multiply by	To Get	Metric System	Symbol
oz.	ounce	28		grams	g
lb.	pounds	0.45		kilograms	kg
	short tons (2000 lb.)	0.9		tonnes	t
tsp.	teaspoons	5		milliliters	ml
tbsp.	tablespoons	15		milliliters	ml
fl. oz.	fluid ounces	30		milliliters	ml
c.	cups	0.24		liters	l
pt.	pints	0.47		liters	l
qt.	quarts	0.95		liters	l
gal.	gallons	3.8		liters	l

Examples: 1.   2 lbs. steak×0.45=.9 kg
                               2.   1 qt. milk×0.95=.95 l
                               3.   1 lb. butter×0.45=.45 kg
                               4.   3 lbs. oranges×0.45=1.35 kg
                               5.   6.8 oz frozen peas ×28=190.4 g

Problems 5–2

Convert to metric system:

(1)   3.75 lbs. pork chops
(2)   4 lbs. apples
(3)   4.7 oz. canned peas
(4)   3.2 oz. deodorant
(5)   3 tsp. margarine
(6)   2 gals. milk
(7)   1 pt. cream cheese
(8)   2 lbs. bacon
(9)   12 tbsp. oil
(10)   50 lbs. sugar

5–3 TEMPERATURE

The kelvin (K) is the standard measure of temperature and is defined as "the temperature of 273.16 degrees or the triple boiling point of water." The temperature K is called "absolute zero." This Celsius or metric temperature is approximately $\frac{5}{9}$ of the Fahrenheit temperature. Celsius temperature is often called "Centigrade" in the U.S. The terms are interchangeable.

Symbol	U.S. System	Multiply by	To Get	Metric System	Symbol
°F	Fahrenheit temperature	$\frac{5}{9}$ (after subtracting 32)		Celsius temperature	°C

Example: What is the normal body temperature in the Celsius system?

$$98.6\degree\,\text{F}. - 32 = 66.6 \times \frac{5}{9}$$

$$= \frac{66.6}{1} \times \frac{5}{9} = 37\degree\,\text{C}.$$

Problems 5–3

Convert the following temperatures for meat, dairy, frozen food cases, etc. to the metric system:

(1) 70°F
(2) 32°F
(3) 60°F
(4) 45°F
(5) 38°F

5–5 METRIC CONVERSION

Conversion to the metric system may be very frustrating for many Americans, and the expense to industry and government will be enormous, but the conversion must be made. In this respect, the U.S. cannot remain out of step with scientific and engineering advances. The change will come gradually; and by using handy tables such as those supplied in this chapter and in the Appendix it may not be as painful as is often feared.

Conversion to the metric system presents both a challenge and an opportunity to American food retailers. The change will make American goods far more attractive and increase sales in world markets. It also should increase international cooperation and expedite the exchange of scientific and medical information.

However, the conversion will be very difficult for many people, who either naturally resist all change or honestly have trouble grasping the new concept. It is here that the food retailer can be quite important because the average person will first feel the conversion in his food shopping. The food retailer faces the challenge of aiding the consumer in understanding the change. Moreover, the food retailer has a unique opportunity to perform a great educational service for his customers and the country. Since most people will learn the metric system in a food store, the retailer should expend every effort to aid in this critical educational process. This is a rare opportunity to serve both customer and community; and the forward-looking company will begin to plan now to take advantage of this situation.

ANSWERS

5–1

Store Q	=	2,880 m²
Selling space	=	2,430 m²
Grocery	=	1,440 m²
Meat	=	270 m²
Produce	=	225 m²

5–2

(1)	1.688 g	(6)	7.6 l
(2)	1.8 kg	(7)	.47 l
(3)	131.6 g	(8)	.9 kg
(4)	89.6 g	(9)	180 ml
(5)	15 ml	(10)	22.5 kg

5–3

(1)	21°C
(2)	0°C
(3)	15.5°C
(4)	7.2°C
(5)	3.3°C

Work Space

Work Space

Work Space

Work Space

6

Simple Relationships

The preceding chapters have covered the basic arithmetic operations for problem solving. This chapter is concerned with some of the simple relationships that will be helpful in solving the problems found in Part III: ratios, proportion, and, most importantly, percentages.

6–1 RATIO AND PROPORTION

The *ratio* of one number to another is the quotient of the first number divided by the second number. Ratio problems involve fractions and, hence, may be solved by the same techniques covered in Chapter 3. When an unknown term has the same ratio to a known term, the unknown can be found by the use of proportion, since *proportion* is really the equality of ratios.

Proportion is usually expressed in this manner, 6: 5:: 12: 10. It is read as, "6 is to 5 as 12 is to 10." This means that 6 has the same ratio to 5 as 12 has to 10. It also means that the ratio of 6 to 5 equals the ratio of 12 to 10.

Problems in proportion are solved by the application of the simple rule, "The product of the means equals the product of the extremes." In a proportion problem, there are four terms: A: B:: C: D. The means are the middle terms or the second and third terms (B,C). The extremes are the outside terms or the first and fourth terms (A,D). Thus,

$$6 : 5 :: 12 : 10$$
$$6 \times 10 = 5 \times 12$$
$$60 = 60$$

This simple procedure can be helpful in many store operations.

Examples:

1. A frozen food department has sales of $4,000 per week, at a net profit of $400. If the produce section has sales of $10,000 per week, what net profit is needed to obtain the same proportional return?

$$\$4,000 : \$400 :: \$10,000 : X$$
$$\$4,000 \times X = \$400 \times \$10,000$$
$$4,000X = \$4,000,000$$
$$X = \$1,000$$

2. The meat manager wants to maintain a 4 to 1 ratio for steaks over roasts. If he has 10 roasts in the counter, how many steaks does he need to maintain the proper ratio?

$$1 : 10 :: 4 : X$$
$$1 \times X = 10 \times 4$$
$$X = 40$$

Problems 6–1

(1) Store A has weekly sales of $100,000, at a labor cost of $20,000. If Store B has sales of $80,000 per week, what labor cost will yield the same proportion?

(2)   Store R has gross sales of $60,000 with a ratio of $8 per square meter. If Store S has sales of $80,000, what sales per square meter figure is needed to yield the same proportion?

(3)   Store C has sales of $40,000 with a ratio of $10,000 sales per register. Store D has sales of $20,000. What amount of sales per register would yield the same proportion?

(4)   Store Y has sales of $10,000 with labor cost at $4,000. Store X has sales of $30,000. What figure for labor cost will yield the same proportion?

6–2 PERCENTAGES

In food store operations, most relationships are expressed in terms of percents. Percents are used to measure the relationships of such components as expenses, costs, sales, and profit between stores, departments, competitors, and managers. The percent is expressed as a percentage of whatever measure is under consideration.

Example: A store has gross sales of $100,000, and produce generates $12,000. What percent of the total sales is attributed to produce?

$$\frac{\$12,000}{\$100,000} = .12 = 12\%$$

Problems 6–2

(1)   Total sales: $146,000
Sales per register: $10,000
Find % per register

(2)   Total sales: $188,000
Sales for frozen food: $9,000
Find % for frozen food

(3)   Total sales: $210,000
Health and beauty aid sales: $6,500
Find % for health and beauty aids

(4)   Total sales: $10,000
       Labor cost: $4,000
       Find % for labor cost
(5)   Total sales: $610,000
       Adminstrative expense: $30,500
       Find % for administrative expense

ANSWERS

6–1

(1) $16,000 labor cost
(2) $10.67 per sq. meter (m²)
(3) $5,000 per register
(4) $12,000 labor cost

6–2

(1)   7%
(2)   5%
(3)   3%
(4)   40%
(5)   5%

Work Space

Work Space

Work Space

Work Space

Part III

Food Store Operating Problems

Part III is concerned with the normal day by day measurements of operating efficiency used in managing a retail food store. The basic arithmetic techniques and relationships discussed in the first two parts of the book should be used to calculate these measures. This section also discusses some problems that occur at the corporate or management level, but these are problems that every store employee should be aware of and be able to calculate. In these cases there will be a clear distinction made between management and store problems; and an explanation as to why they are important to the store employee will be included.

We begin with a simplified, basic store operating statement from which almost all operating data and problems are derived. Then, the following specific areas are discussed and analyzed:

- Markups and Margins: The methods by which the final retail selling price is determined based on the cost of an item.
- Inventory Control: The major store control problem of maintaining the least possible inventory without having "out-of-stock" situations.
- Turnover: The most helpful measure of how efficiently inventory is being maintained.

- Markdowns and Discounting: The fairly simple but very important process of reducing prices for merchandising or competitive reasons.
- Discounts: The price discounts received from the stores' suppliers.
- Unit Pricing: The now almost universally accepted concept of quoting the price of an item in its most commonly expressed quantity or unit in order to help the consumer make more relevant price and quality comparisons.
- Open Dating: The emerging concept of placing simple, easy-to-read expiration dates on all food products.
- Nutritional Labeling: The printing of complete nutritional information on the labels of food products.
- Sales Taxes: The retail sales tax charged in many states and cities.
- Elimination of Price Changes: The new concept in food retailing, in which no price change is allowed once an item is on the shelf.
- Laws and Regulations: The various legal areas confronting the retail store employee.
- Universal Product Code: This is perhaps the most important innovation in food retailing in 30 years, the complete code identification system for all food products.
- Wage Calculation: The fairly simple task of computing a workers' wages.
- Job Scheduling: The more complex problem of the proper scheduling of employees.
- Operating Ratios: The many helpful measures of operating data.

The book concludes with a chapter of practical supermarket arithmetic problems.

7

Operating Statements and Gross Margin

A store's operating statement is, of course, calculated at the corporate or company management level. However, since it is the basic operating document for the store, it is desirable for each employee to understand it, and what it can tell him about his company's business.

The sample statements used here are purposely brief, leaving out accounting details that will be of little interest to a store employee. A standard accounting text may be consulted for more detailed analysis.

There are six terms the store person should be concerned with in the operating statement: (1) gross sales, (2) cost of goods sold, (3) gross margin, (4) labor expenses, (5) other expenses, and (6) net profit.

Gross Sales is the total dollar sales figure in the store for a specific period of time, such as a week, a quarter, or a year.

Cost of Goods Sold is the dollar value of the merchandise sold by the store during the same time period. This figure is usually adjusted to allow for beginning and ending inventory. As a national average, cost of goods sold is generally around 80 percent of gross sales. This figure will vary depending on many factors such as type of operation, union or non-union store, and geographic location.

A typical store operating statement would look like this:

		Amount	Percentage
Gross Sales		$504,000	100.0%
−Cost of Goods Sold		$405,000	80.4%
Gross Margin		$ 99,000	19.6%
Labor Expense	$42,000		
Other Expense	$38,000		
Total Expense	$80,000		
−Total Expense		$ 80,000	15.9%
Net Profit		$ 19,000	3.7%

Gross Margin is the difference between gross sales and cost of goods sold, and is estimated at about 20 percent for a national average.[1]

Gross Sales	$100,000
−Cost of Goods Sold	−$ 80,000
Gross Margin	$ 20,000

Expenses are usually shown in great detail on an operating statement and include factors such as rent, light, heat, power, license fees, insurance, interest, legal fees, and depreciation. For

---

[1] Theodore Leed and Gene German, *Food Merchandising* (New York, Chain Store Publishing Corp., 1973), p. 169.

purposes of this section, we will simply use the two general categories of *Labor Expenses* and *Other Expenses*. Together, these types of expenses may average between 15 and 19 percent of gross margin, depending again on type of operation, labor cost, and geographic location.

Net Profit, the so-called "Bottom Line," is the key to all free enterprise. Without some level of profit, the enterprise cannot survive, workers are unemployed, and the process of food distribution is broken. Net profit as a percent of sales for food stores has been averaging one percent or less for corporate chains and four percent or slightly higher for independent operators.

	Gross Margin	$20,000
Labor Expense $10,000		
Other Expenses $8,000		
	− Total Expenses	$18,000
	Net Profit	$ 2,000

It should be emphasized here that the one to four percent net profit average for food retailers is considerably lower than that for most other American businesses.[2] The food store employee should keep in mind that the one percent profit figure can vanish rather quickly as a result of what might be a minor mistake or miscalculation such as a mis-ring on a cash register or an improper store order.

Problems

(1) Stores A and B are similar-size units of a corporate chain in similar neighborhoods. Calculate a brief operating statement for each and show which is more efficient and why.

Store A: gross sales, $812,000; cost of goods sold, $644,000; labor expense, $82,000; other expenses, $79,000.

---

[2] *Operating Results of Food Chains* (Ithaca, N.Y.: Cornell University, 1973).

Store B: gross sales, $808,000; cost of goods sold, $636,000; labor expenses, $83,800; other expenses, $80,000.

(2) Store P and Store Q are similar size units with similar locations. Store P has gross sales of $700,000; cost of goods sold, $622,000; labor expense, $40,000; other expense, $36,000. Store Q has gross sales of $680,000; cost of goods sold, $590,000; labor expense, $56,000; other expenses, $30,000. Calculate their operating statements and account for any differences.

(3) Stores X and Y are fairly similar units of the same voluntary organization. Calculate a brief operating statement for each; and show which is more efficient and why.

Store X: gross sales, $212,000; cost of goods sold, $161,000; total expenses, $38,000.

Store Y: gross sales, $224,000; cost of goods sold $184,000; total expenses, $34,000.

ANSWERS

Store A

(1)			
Gross Sales		$812,000	100.0%
− Cost of Goods Sold		− $644,000	− 79.3%
Gross Margin		$168,000	20.7%
Labor Expense	$ 82,000		
Other Expense	$ 79,000		
Total Expense	$161,000		
Gross Margin		$168,000	20.7%
− Total Expense		− $161,000	− 19.8%
Net Profit		$ 7,000	.9%

Store B

Gross Sales		$808,000	100.0%
− Cost of Goods Sold		− $636,000	− 78.7%
Gross Margin		$172,000	21.3%
Labor Expense	$ 83,800		
Other Expense	$ 80,000		
Total Expense	$163,800		
Gross Margin		$172,000	21.3%
− Total Expense		− $163,800	− 20.3%
Net Profit		$ 8,200	1.0%

Store B is a slightly more efficient operation on the basis of net profit difference, but there are some internal differences between the stores that are equally interesting. Store A has slightly higher gross sales, which is not too important since this could be caused by many factors beyond the store manager's control. The lower cost of goods sold figure for Store B is more important. Since both stores belong to the same corporate chain, their warehouse delivery costs should be the same. But it is possible that Store A is not being careful enough in monitoring vendors who make store-door deliveries. This area is often overlooked as a possible place where costs can be reduced.

Store A has a lower "other" expense figure, which again may be attributed to external factors. However, the high labor expense figure for Store B may indicate too much overtime or improper work scheduling which is an internal problem. These two stores, similar in purpose, were chosen for this problem in order to show how, even under similar conditions, slight oversights can affect profits for a company and perhaps bonuses and promotions for employees.

		Store P		**Store Q**	
(2)	Gross Sales	$700,000	100.0%	$680,000	100.0%
	−Cost of Goods Sold	$622,000	89.0%	$590,000	86.8%
	Gross Margin	$ 78,000	11.0%	$ 90,000	13.2%
	−Labor Expense	$ 40,000	5.7%	$ 56,000	8.2%
	−Other Expense	$ 36,000	5.0%	$ 30,000	4.4%
	Net Profit	$ 2,000	0.3%	$ 4,000	0.6%

Both stores have a high cost of goods sold figure which makes profitable operation difficult for each. Store Q shows a slightly better net profit because of its control over other expenses; but neither store is in a strong position.

		Store X		**Store Y**	
(3)	Gross Sales	$212,000	100.0%	$224,000	100.0%
	−Cost of Goods Sold	$161,000	75.9%	$184,000	82.1%
	Gross Margin	$ 51,000	24.1%	$ 40,000	17.9%
	−Total Expenses	$ 38,000	17.9%	$ 34,000	15.2%
	Net Profit	$ 13,000	6.2%	$ 6,000	2.7%

This problem shows considerably more contrast between stores than earlier ones. Store Y has higher sales, but a much lower net profit. The difference is, of course, in the cost of goods sold category. Store Y must have a very different product mix than Store X. Also, Store Y may be carrying more expensive items with lower profit margins.

Work Space

Work Space

Work Space

Work Space

8

Markups and Margins

8–1

The final selling prices of products in a retail store generally are arrived at by adding a certain percentage *markup* or *margin* to the cost of each item. This percentage markup is designed to cover the cost of the store's operations and to allow, of course, for profit. Markup, then, is simply the difference between cost and selling price and includes the net profit. (See Chapter 7).

$$\text{Markup} = \text{Selling Price} - \text{Cost}$$

However, markup is usually expressed as a percentage of cost:

$$\% \text{ Markup} = \frac{\text{Selling Price} - \text{Cost}}{\text{Cost}} \times 100$$

which gives the ratio of selling price to cost of goods. The markup obviously varies from item to item and from store to store, depending on cost, selling price, and the profit objectives of management.

Example: A case of canned tomatoes (12 pack)
                          costs $3.80, and sells for $.39 per can. Cal-
                          culate markup and percent markup.
                          Cost $3.80
                          Selling Price   12×.39=$4.68
                          Markup=$4.68−$3.80=$ .88
                          $$\% \text{ Markup} = \frac{\$4.68 - \$3.80}{\$3.80} = \frac{\$ .88}{\$3.80}$$
                          $$= .23 = 23\%$$

Problems 8–1

Calculate Markup and % Markup:

(1)   Frozen green beans: Cost, $3.98   Selling Price, $4.85
(2)   Liquid detergent: Cost, $12.84   Selling Price, $15.50
(3)   Box matches (12 pack): Cost, $.89   Selling Price, $.09 each
(4)   Prime ribs: Cost, $1.60 lb.   Selling Price, $1.99 lb.
(5)   Sugar: Cost, $2.15 for 5 lbs.   Selling Price, $2.95 for
                                             5 lbs.
(6)   Bread: Cost, $.25 for 1 loaf   Selling Price, $.38 for 1
                                             loaf

8–2

Although most retailers arrive at their prices by using a
markup system, the majority of food retailers are somewhat unique
in that they use a "margin" or "gross margin" calculation instead of
markup. This difference might be confusing to an employee who
has recently transferred from non-food to food retailing.

Gross margin, like markup, is the difference between cost and
selling price:

$$\text{Gross Margin} = \text{Selling Price} - \text{Cost}$$

However, the *percent margin* is different from the *percent markup:*

$$\% \text{ Margin} = \frac{\text{Selling Price} - \text{Cost}}{\text{Selling Price}} \times 100$$

Example: A case of canned tomatoes (12 pack) costs $3.80 and is sold for $.39 per can. Calculate margin and % margin.

Cost $3.80

Selling Price $12 \times \$.39 = \$4.68$

Margin $= \$4.68 - \$3.80 = \$.88$

$$\% \text{ Margin} = \frac{\$4.68 - \$3.80}{\$4.68} = \frac{\$.88}{\$4.68} = 18.8\%$$

Note this example compared with the example in section 8–1: the dollar difference is the same; it is the percent difference that varies. The margin percent is always lower than the markup percent because the denominator is always larger.

Problems 8–2

Calculate Margin and % Margin:

(1) Frozen green beans: Cost, $3.98   Selling Price, $4.85

(2) Liquid detergent: Cost, $12.84   Selling Price, $15.50

(3) Frozen pizza (12 pack): Cost,
     $11.15 case   Selling Price, $1.19 each

(4) Canned corn (24 pack): Cost,
     $3.98 case   Selling Price, $.19 each

(5) Sugar: Cost, $2.15 for 5 lbs.   Selling Price, $2.95 for 5 lbs.

(6) Bread: Cost, $.25 for 1 loaf   Selling Price, $.38 for 1 loaf

8–3

Although gross margin is commonly used to project profit percentage, it may also be used to calculate the selling price, if the desired margin is used.

$$\text{Selling Price} = \frac{\text{Cost}}{100\% - \% \text{ margin desired}}$$

Example: ABC Markets buys frozen green beans at $3.60 per case, and would like to achieve a gross margin of $33\frac{1}{3}\%$ on this item. Calculate the selling price.

$$\text{Selling Price} = \frac{\$3.60}{100\% - 33.3\%} = \frac{\$3.60}{.667}$$
$$= \$5.40 \text{ case}$$

Problems 8–3

Calculate selling price:

(1) Canned dog food: Cost, $.19   Desired Margin, 33%
(2) Frozen peas: Cost, $.89   Desired Margin, 27%
(3) Fresh bananas: Cost, $.08   Desired Margin, 18%
(4) Ground beef: Cost, $.99   Desired Margin, 25%
(5) Baby food: Cost, $.49   Desired Margin, 15%
(6) Stockings: Cost, $1.00   Desired Margin, 50%

8–4

Leed and German make a very important point—that it may be quite helpful for the store employee to be able to convert quickly from percent markup to percent margin since this type of calculation is necessary at certain times.[1]

$$\% \text{ Margin} = \frac{\% \text{ Markup}}{100\% + \% \text{ Markup}}$$

Example: If % Markup is 50%, what is the % Margin?

$$\% \text{ Margin} = \frac{50}{100 + 50} = \frac{50}{150} 33\frac{1}{3}\%$$

---

[1] Leed, German, *Food Merchandising*, p. 110.

Problems 8–4

Calculate % Margin, if % Markup is:

(1)   10%
(2)   25%
(3)   30%
(4)   40%
(5)   50%
(6)   35%
(7)   15%

8–5

There are two major points which should be made clear in dealing with markups and margins. The margin figure is always lower than the markup percentage, simply because of the nature of the calculation. Although this difference may be obvious, some food retailers mis-use this fact by arguing that they do not mark up as much as non-food retailers. This is not a valid argument and can only hurt the retailer's image in the long run.

The second point is that margins vary dramatically from store to store, department to department, and item to item. It is, therefore, difficult to relate margin to profit in many cases. A frozen food department, for example, may have a high percent margin, but a low volume or a low percentage of store sales, and therefore does not contribute much to store profit. On the other hand, the grocery department may have a lower percent margin, but because of high volume, contributes more to store profits.

Some traditional supermarket items called "loss leaders" (coffee for one) might be sold at a very low margin or perhaps even at a loss. This is sometimes done as part of a store's overall merchandising policy.

ANSWERS

8–1

(1)	$ .87 markup	21.8%
(2)	$2.66 markup	20.7%
(3)	$ .19 markup	21.3%
(4)	$ .39 markup	24.4%
(5)	$ .80 markup	37.2%
(6)	$ .13 markup	52%

8–2

(1)	$ .87 margin	17.9%
(2)	$2.66 margin	17.2%
(3)	$3.13 margin	21.9%
(4)	$ .58 margin	12.7%
(5)	$ .80 margin	27%
(6)	$ .13 margin	34.2%

8–3

(1)	$ .28
(2)	$1.22
(3)	$ .10
(4)	$1.32
(5)	$ .58
(6)	$2.00

8–4

(1)	9%
(2)	20%
(3)	23%
(4)	29%
(5)	$33\frac{1}{3}$%
(6)	26%
(7)	13%

Work Space

Work Space

Work Space

Work Space

9

Inventory Control and Turnover

9-1 INVENTORY MANAGEMENT

Inventory management has always been an area of major concern to food retailers, but in recent years there has been increasing pressure on store managers and employees to control inventory more effectively. Although every store and company uses its own inventory control system, each system involves the principle of least cost, or the attempt to maintain the lowest possible inventory without creating out-of-stock situations. This is a most delicate balance indeed.

The problem of inventory control has increased for several reasons:

- Most retail food stores have decreased their in-store inventory and are attempting to rely on improved warehouse delivery systems.
- The out-of-stock problem has caused major complaints from consumer groups.

- The out-of-stock problem, when tied to retail advertising, has created many legal problems. At times, food stores have been prosecuted for failing to have an advertised item in stock. Out-of-stocks can be the result of any number of uncontrollable factors such as delayed delivery, careless shelf stocking, poor communication from the main office, or even a sell-out as the result of a successful merchandise program. However, in several cases, stores have still been held legally responsible for false advertising. The Federal Trade Commission has indicated that the use of "rainchecks" does not absolve the store of the responsibility for not having the item on hand.

The adoption of the Universal Product Code and Optical Scan Checkouts (see Chapter 11) will improve this situation dramatically, but the pressure on the store manager probably will continue into the foreseeable future. This is an area in which the good manager can make a major impression on management by his ability to keep close control over inventory.

9–2 TURNOVER

The speed with which the average stock or inventory in a department or store is sold is referred to as *turnover*. Turnover is a fairly simple and yet major measure of operating efficiency. All things being equal, the faster items are sold, the less stock is maintained, and the less capital is required. Therefore, the faster the rate of turnover, the more efficient the operation.

Turnover is a fairly simple calculation. It is found by dividing the sales in a given period by the average inventory for the area in question. Turnover is always shown as a whole or decimal number and is not expressed in dollars or percentages.

$$\text{Turnover} = \frac{\text{Sales}}{\text{Average Inventory}}$$

Example: The produce department of XYZ Food Store has yearly sales of $280,000, with an average inventory of $40,000. What is the rate of turnover?

$$\text{Turnover} = \frac{\$280,000}{\$40,000} = 7.00 \text{ turns per year}$$

Problems 9–2

(1) A grocery department has sales of $1,879,628 per year, with an average inventory of $829,000. Find turnover.

(2) Store W has yearly sales of $226,000, with an average inventory of $112,000. Find turnover.

(3) A deli department has sales of $960 per week with an average inventory of $426. Find weekly turnover.

(4) Store K has sales of $114,000 per year with an average inventory of $63,000. Store Y has sales of $124,000 with an average inventory of $78,000. Compare turnovers.

(5) Store A has yearly sales of $1,112,000, with an average inventory of $379,000. Store B has yearly sales of $1,383,000 with an average inventory of $468,000. Which store is making better use of inventory control?

(6) Store Y has yearly sales of $1,250,000 with an average inventory of $550,000. Find turnover.

(7) Store Z has yearly sales of $625,000, with an average inventory of $125,000. Find turnover.

ANSWERS

9–2

(1)   2.27 turns per year
(2)   2.02 turns per year
(3)   2.25 turns per week
(4)   Store K: 1.81 turns per year
      Store Y: 1.59 turns per year
      Store K has a more rapid turnover
(5)   Store A: 2.93 turns per year
      Store B: 2.96 turns per year
      Store B has a marginally faster turnover rate and would be considered slightly more efficient.
(6)   2.27 turns per year
(7)   5.0 turns per year

Work Space

Work Space

Work Space

Work Space

10

Discounts and Discounting

Discounts are reductions from the seller's normal retail price. Because of the food retailer's low profit margin (see Chapter 7), the many different types of discounts available are very important to him.

Discounting, or the general reduction of most prices in the entire store, is a marketing strategy which was widely developed and emphasized by food retailers during the early 1970s.

10–1 DISCOUNTS

Food manufacturers and processors make many types of discounts and allowances available to food retailers, and these can be very important to a firm's profit structure. Although these discounts usually are handled at the corporate level, it is important for the store employee to understand the mechanics of discounts.

Cash discounts are a slight reduction from the normal price. They are designed to encourage the buyer to pay in cash and to pay quickly. Cash discounts generally are shown in some abbreviated form:

- *2/10, n/30* means a two percent discount if the bill is paid within 10 days and net amount (n) due in 30 days.
- *5/10, 2/30* means a five percent discount if the bill is paid within 10 days or a two percent discount if paid within 30 days.
- *E.O.M.* refers to end of the month dating and might read "4/10, EOM," with a four percent cash discount in the first 10 days and the net amount due in 30 days or at the end of the month.
- *R.O.G.* is similar to E.O.M., and refers to receipt of goods dating. It might read "4/10, ROG," with a four percent cash discount in the first 10 days after delivery, with the net amount due in either 20 or 30 days.

Food retailers should take advantage of every cash discount that is offered. In an industry where profits run as low as one percent, any discount can be critical to success.

Various *trade or functional discounts* are granted to buyers who are in different positions in the trade or marketing channel of distribution. These discounts are based on the number of economic functions each buyer performs. Thus, if a retailer and a wholesaler buy from the same manufacturer, they each receive a different discount depending on their respective positions in the marketing channel and the diverse services or functions they perform. All things being equal, the more services the buyer performs for the seller, such as transport or storage, the higher the discount he will receive.

For example, if two stores buy the same quantity from a manufacturer, they pay the same price. But, if one store has the item delivered and the other goes to the plant and picks it up, the store that performs its own transport function receives a lower price or a larger trade or functional discount.

Quantity discounts are perhaps the most common of all discounts, yet they are also the most confusing and sometimes raise serious legal questions. The 1936 Robinson-Patman Act was designed to restrict the excessive buying power of large retailers. Quantity discounts are permittted under this law; but either the buyer or seller or both must be able to prove that a quantity discount is based on legitimate cost-saving since this type of discount cannot be given just because one buyer is larger and more powerful than others.

Generally, the law requires that a quantity discount must be made available to all buyers in proportion to what they purchase. The size of the discount may vary depending on cost differences such as higher or lower delivery charges, storage costs, or billing costs. The Robinson-Patman Act, however, is unclear in many ways and is a constant source of concern for food retailers.

Advertising allowances are similar to quantity discounts in that the buyer receives a certain amount of cooperative advertising money from the seller, and this acts as an extra discount from the usual price of the goods. Under the Robinson-Patman Act, advertising allowances also must be made available to all buyers in proportion to the amount they purchase.

Free goods are additional quantities of merchandise offered to a retailer at no cost, if he has already purchased a certain amount of that item. For example, a retailer may get one free case of an item if he purchases 10 cases. Again, free goods constitute a quantity discount, and, by law, must be made available to all buyers on a proportional basis. Free goods are especially important at the store level because it is possible for an over-eager store employee to talk a salesman into giving extra free goods, an act that could be in violation of the Robinson-Patman law.

10–2 DISCOUNTING

Discounting is a term used to describe retail promotional efforts that emphasize low prices. A major form of competition in food retailing during the early 1970s, discounting replaced the non-price competition that dominated food retailing for two decades prior to that. During the 1950s and 1960s, the major marketing emphasis was on service, quality, reliability, and promotions such as coupons, premiums, trading stamps, and games of chance.

At the end of the 1960s, the rising rate of inflation and increased pressure from consumers led eventually to discounting on a large scale in food stores. The discounting wave led to a series of supermarket price wars in some areas and a great reduction in non-price competition techniques such as stamps, games, and coupons. The discounting took several forms, with some stores lowering all their prices and others emphasizing only certain selected items. Some stores changed their names to appear more discount-oriented; others merely changed their promotional image.

There has been very little research into just what discounting really involves. The best information is from a study of food store discounting in Denver, Colorado.[1] The Denver study maintains that a discount price should be at least two percent lower than the previous price, or the consumer will be unaware of the difference. The study also indicates that the discount should not exceed five percent on all discounted items, or the retailer will lose profits.

Discounts or *markdowns* usually are administered from the main office of a food chain in the form of price change directives, but it is important for the store employee to be able to make such calculations quickly and easily and to understand them.

$$\text{Discount} = \text{Original Price} - \text{New Selling Price}$$

$$\% \text{ Discount} = \frac{\text{Discount}}{\text{New Selling Price}}$$

Example: Canned peas are reduced from \$.39 to \$.37. Calculate discount and % discount.

$$\text{Discount} = \$.39 - \$.37 = \$.02$$

$$\% \text{ Discount} = \frac{\$.02}{\$.37} = 5.4\%$$

---

[1] Eugene Beem, *Turmoil in the Supermarket Industry,* (Denver: American Marketing Association, December, 1968).

Problems 10–2

Calculate % discount:

(1) Frozen Waffles $.89 to $.83
(2) Eggs $.99 doz. to $.89 doz.
(3) Ice Cream $.69 per ½ gal. to $.39 per ½ gal.
(4) Turkeys $.59 lb. to $.49 lb.
(5) Jelly $.49 to $.44
(6) Chocolate Cookies $.89 to $.69

10–3 SELLING PRICE

It also may be helpful for the store employee to be able to calculate the new selling price if he knows the desired discount percent. To do this, multiply the original selling price by the percent discount desired, and subtract the result from the original selling price.

Example: Potatoes are selling for $.99 for 5 lbs. A five-percent discount is desired. Calculate new selling price:

$$\$.99 \times .05 = \$.05$$
$$\$.99 - \$.05 = \$.94 \text{ new price}$$

Problems 10–3

P-L Markets wishes to discount all merchandise by four percent. Calculate the new prices.

(1) $ .89
(2) $ .79
(3) $ 1.19
(4) $12.57
(5) $ .09
(6) $ .52
(7) $ .21

ANSWERS

10–2

(1)   7.2%
(2)   11.2%
(3)   76.9%
(4)   20.4%
(5)   11.3%
(6)   28.9%

10–3

(1) $ .85
(2) $ .76
(3) $ 1.14
(4) $12.07
(5) $ .08
(6) $ .50
(7) $ .20

Work Space

Work Space

Work Space

Work Space

11

Unit Pricing and
Other Consumer Aids

This chapter is concerned first with the fairly simple arithmetic calculations that are involved in unit pricing; then, several other current changes taking place in food retailing are considered.

11-1 UNIT PRICING

The consumer movement of the 1960s gave rise to a need for *unit pricing* of products sold in retail food stores. Unit pricing is designed to help consumers make meaningful price comparisons between brands and sizes of products based upon standard units of weight or measure. It is required by law in a few states and the District of Columbia. More importantly, over 100 food chains voluntarily have adopted unit pricing.

Unit pricing in a strict sense simply refers to the practice of selling each item as an individual unit and not on a multiple-unit basis. The most important part of unit pricing is the concept of *price by measure*. This is the method by which the price is calculated in relation to some normally-accepted quantity or measure in order to allow the consumer to make more meaningful price and quality comparisons.

Although the unit price calculation usually is made at corporate headquarters and arrives at the store in label form, it is important for the store person to be able to make a quick calculation in order to check for errors or to explain a price to a questioning customer.

The unit price label on the package or shelf, or both, usually looks something like this:

SIZE	**ITEM**	**BRAND**
16 oz.	Canned Peas	X
PRICE THIS ITEM		**UNIT PRICE**
2 for $.47		$.24 per lb.

11–1 Problems

Calculate unit price:

(1)	5 lb. potatoes	at $ .79
(1a)	10 lbs.	at $ .69
(2)	2 doz. potatoes	at $1.69
(3)	Margarine—2 lbs.	at $ .99
(3a)	1 lb.	at $ .59
(4)	3.5 lbs. steak	at $4.85
(5)	12 oz. cleaning fluid	at $ .79
(5a)	24 oz.	at $1.40
(6)	5 lbs. detergent	at $2.89

11–2 OPEN DATING

Open dating is the process of placing on all food products an expiration date that is easy to read and understand. Food manufacturers and retailers always have dated the expected shelf life of most products, but the codes used were often confusing, if not unintelligible. The consumer's dissatisfaction with these obsolete codes has led to a move in the food industry toward new and more understandable codes. Several types of codes have been suggested:

- A pack date showing the day the product received final manufacture or packaging.

- A display date giving the date the product first went on the retail shelf.

- An expiration date indicating that the product is of unacceptable quality beyond that date.

- A quality assurance date showing the date beyond which the quality will begin to fade.

- A pull date giving the last date the item should be sold in the retail store, or the day it should be "pulled" from the shelf.

Most companies now agree that the pull date concept is the most acceptable for all parties. It has been implemented by many food manufacturers on a voluntary basis.

11-3 NUTRITIONAL LABELING

Consumer groups also have complained about the lack of nutritional information on the labels of food products. As a result, many food manufacturers are now adding nutritional information to their labels on a voluntary basis. The sample below reflects the kind of information that can be found on a typical cereal package.

NUTRITION INFORMATION PER SERVING

SERVING SIZE: One ounce (1 cup) of cereal in combination with ½ cup vitamin D fortified whole milk.

SERVINGS PER CONTAINER: 11

	1 oz.	with ½ cup of whole milk
Calories	120	200
Protein	1 gm	6 gm
Carbohydrates	25 gm	31 gm
Fat	1 gm	6 gm

PERCENTAGE OF U. S. RECOMMENDED DAILY ALLOWANCE (U.S.D.A.)

	1 oz.	with ½ cup of whole milk
Protein	2	10
Vitamin A	20	20
Vitamin C	25	25
Thiamine	25	25
Riboflavin	25	35
Niacin	30	30
Calcium	*	15
Iron	10	10
Vitamin D	5	30
Vitamin B_6	25	25
Folic Acid	25	25
Phosphorus	2	10
Magnesium	*	4

* Contains less than two percent of the U.S.D.A. daily requirements of these nutrients.

INGREDIENTS: Sugar, corn, wheat and oat flour, salt, certified colors, and natural fruit flavoring with vitamin A, sodium ascorbate, thiamine (B_1), riboflavin (B_2), niacinamide, vitamin D, pyridoxine (B_6), folic acid and iron phosphate added. BHA and BHT added to preserve product freshness.

Nutritional labeling, a voluntary program prior to January 1, 1975, is now compulsory for all products that are processed and packaged and shipped interstate, with any claims as to nutritional value. Even a very simple claim, such as "better for children," requires a nutritional information disclosure on the label.

11-4 SALES TAXES

Many states and cities have a retail sales tax which can create several problems for store personnel:

- Although the tax is usually stated as a percentage (four percent, five percent, etc.), it generally cannot be calculated directly, because there is usually some exemption (the first 10 cents, 20 cents, etc.). Therefore, store employees must rely on the tax table provided by their state tax agency. (See Appendix.)
- Although many foods are not subject to sales taxes, some items in a food store are taxable, depending on the state laws. This is often very confusing to new employees, especially checkers. The choice of taxable items by the state is often capricious at best (e.g.—fruit juice may not be taxable, while fruit drink may be).
- The retail store becomes the collection agency for the state; this adds many responsibilities on the already burdened store manager.
- The retail sales tax is clearly regressive in that the burden of the tax falls most heavily on those who can least afford to pay.
- The tax is harmful to retailers in one area if an adjoining state or city does not have a sales tax. Pennsylvania and New Jersey are good examples, with New Jersey's lower sales tax inducing many Philadelphians to shop across the Delaware.

11-5 PRICE CHANGES

The most commonly heard of all complaints against food retailers concerns excessive price changes (increases) in the store itself. Most stores are now adopting a "no price change" policy. This means that the price of an item will not be increased after it reaches the retail shelf. Although this is good for consumers, it may confuse them for awhile because there may be two of the same item on a shelf with different prices; and the manager should be patient in explaining the process.

11–6 MAKING CHANGE

One of the more simple and yet annoying problems of food retailing is the physical act of making change. Although many new cash registers calculate the customer's change automatically, in many stores, the clerk must make his own mental calculation.

There are two standard techniques used to calculate change. In the negative technique, the clerk subtracts the cost of the order from the amount of money provided by the customer. In the positive approach, the clerk adds from the cost of the order until he arrives at the amount received from the customer. Most stores prefer the positive approach for two reasons: addition is a slightly easier calculation for most people than subtraction, and the positive approach allows the customer to "see" and understand the calculation.

11–7 LAWS AND REGULATIONS

There are many areas of regulation and legal problems that involve mathematical calculations, and they can cause problems for the store manager. The following are some areas of concern:

- *Licenses and Inspection* A retail food store is usually required to have several different types of operating licenses, which are usually followed by some inspection process such as checks on weights and scales, sanitation, fire protection, etc.
- *Weights and Measures* The manager is responsible for all weighing and measuring equipment, which is often very sensitive and difficult to keep in good working order.

- *Alcohol and Tobacco Laws* There are so many varia-
  tions in these areas, it is impossible to list them here.
  However, they always are a problem for the manager.

- *USDA Food Stamps* These again are an annoyance to
  the store manager, since the regulations are confusing and
  constantly changing. But they are a source of store income and are most helpful to low income citizens.

- Just a brief list of other possible legal areas would
  include:

  > Labor union violations and grievances
  > Accidents to customers or employees
  > Sanitation violations
  > Blue laws
  > Packaging and labeling laws
  > Fair trade laws
  > Narcotics and dangerous drug laws
  > Counterfeit money
  > Fire protection
  > Police protection
  > Occupational Safety and Health Administration
  > (OSHA)
  > Environmental Protection Agency (EPA)
  > Product safety

11–8 UNIVERSAL PRODUCT CODE

The *Universal Product Code* is an optical scan mark designed
to be read by a lazer beam which translates the code to an in-store
computer. The codes were adopted after consultation with repre-
sentatives from all areas of the food industry. Every product sold
in a food store must have its own distinctive code. The code is
meant to be read by the scanning device, not by the human eye.

In the Universal Product Code, the first five digits identify
the manufacturer and the second five the item, so that all products
will have a unique code.

Manufacturers Label

Some stores may use a 12-digit code system in departments such as meat where more information is needed by the retailer.

Other stores, at least for awhile, may use a combination code and price symbol in departments such as produce.

The Universal Product Code does not contain the price. The price information is stored in mini-checkout computers, recorded in the store's computer, and printed on the customer's tape when the optical scanner reads the code on each item. This system has many advantages to both retailers and consumers.

For the consumer, (a) there is no danger of the item being mispriced, or not corrected for price changes; (b) it eliminates fear of mistakes by the checkout person.

For the retailer, (a) it eliminates the enormous cost of pricing each item, although at least one state is considering a regulation that would demand that both the code and the price appear on each item (such a law probably would destroy almost all of the cost-saving features of the code); (b) it provides almost instant and completely accurate inventory control, which may be the greatest advantage.

The cost of the systems needed to implement the Universal Product Code is very high; and it may be some years before it is fully adopted. But, it should be beneficial to food companies and consumers alike. Many firms already are using the code on their products; and a few stores have installed computers to make full use of the code. It appears, however, that total adoption is some years away.

ANSWERS

11–1

(1) $ .16 per lb.
(1a) $ .07 per lb.
(2) $ .84½ per doz.
(3) $ .49½ per lb.
(3a) $ .59 per lb.
(4) $1.38½ per lb.
(5) $ .06½ per oz.
(5a) $ .06 per oz.
(6)   · $ .58 per lb.

Work Space

Work Space

Work Space

Work Space

12

Payroll and Work Scheduling

Although the areas of payroll and scheduling are becoming more and more the responsibility of the personnel manager or labor relations director, it is still very important for store people to understand the basis of employee compensation and job scheduling. Also, since labor costs account for 50 percent of all expenses or 10 percent of gross sales, this is a most important area of potential cost saving which leads to increased net profit.

12–1 PAYROLL

Employee compensation is ordinarily based either on time or productivity. The time basis is almost universally used in food retailing. Wages are usually paid weekly in food stores and are based on an hourly rate. Most employees have a normal number of hours to work per week on straight time. Their total wage, then, is simply the hourly pay rate times the number of hours.

$$\text{Wage} = \text{rate per hour} \times \text{hours worked}$$
$$\$80 = \$2 \text{ per hour} \times 40 \text{ hours}$$

Some employees may work more hours than they are normally scheduled in which case they are often paid an overtime hourly rate. This makes the calculation slightly more difficult.

Wage = regular hour rate × regular hours worked +
overtime hour rate × overtime hours worked
$110.00 = $2.00 per hour × 40 hours + $3.00 per hour × 10 hours

The overtime rates may vary depending on the number of hours worked or because of different hourly shifts or special work days, such as Sundays or holidays. Employee hours usually are calculated by some kind of time clock device.

Example: A checkout clerk receives $3.80 per hour for the first 40 hours, and time and a half pay for 12 hours of regular overtime, plus double time for eight hours on Sunday. Calculate wage.

Wage = 40 hours × $3.80 = $152.00
12 hours × $5.70 = $ 68.40
8 hours × $7.60 = $ 60.80
                                $281.20

Problems 12–1

Calculate wages:

(1)   Retail Clerk: 40 hours at $4.24; 10 hours overtime at time and a half; 12 hours at double time.
(2)   Meat Cutter: 37.5 hours at $6.24; 10 hours at double time; 10 hours at triple time.
(3)   Stock Clerk: 48 hours at $2.12; 10 hours overtime at $2.50.
(4)   Cashier: 40 hours at $3.75; 10 hours overtime at time and a half.
(5)   Frozen Food Clerk: 35 hours at $2.50; four hours overtime at $3.00.

12–2 SCHEDULING

Although the store manager receives considerable help from the main office on wages and deductions, he is often solely responsible for work schedules, and may be very carefully evaluated on how well he uses his work force (see Chapter 13).

There are many factors about scheduling that the good manager should keep in mind:

- Always consider when the overtime rate begins. Although the straight time rate is 40 hours, the overtime rate may not begin until 45 hours. Thus, the manager has five hours per employee to work with at straight time.
- The overtime rate may be less for part-time than for full-time employees.
- The overtime rate may jump in stages at 45 hours, 50 hours, etc. The manager should try to schedule below each jump.
- Part-time employees in some areas are paid considerably less than full-time, and thus are used to keep down total wages.
- Even where part-time and full-time wages are the same, the part-time employee may receive fewer fringe benefits and thus is used more.
- The labor force should be as small as possible on special rate days or hours without hurting store efficiency.
- If there are both union and non-union workers in a store, or two different unions, this might alter the scheduling procedure.
- The manager is generally not concerned with fringe benefits; therefore, it is the responsibility of the employee to be certain he receives all the benefits he is entitled to. The manager should be able to answer questions in these areas, however.

In all cases, the manager is attempting to balance the best possible use of the labor force versus the lowest possible total wage bill. This is a difficult and delicate balance. Today with rapidly rising labor costs, many food stores admit they are willing to sacrifice labor efficiency in order to keep down labor costs.

The manager should remember that unfair scheduling can be a violation of the Fair Labor Standards Act or perhaps a Civil Rights violation with respect to age, sex, race, or national origin. A special problem is the over-use of young people, which can lead to child labor law violations.

Edward Harwell's book, *Checkout Management,* offers the best coverage of employee scheduling; his Chapter 6 is required reading for anyone concerned with this area.[1]

A typical food store schedule chart for clerks and baggers might look like the following:

Employee Scheduled	Full Time	Part Time	10-11	11-12	12-1	1-2	2-3	3-4	Total
#8327	X		C	C	L	C	C	C	5
#1652	X		C	L	C	C	C	C	5
#1227	X		C	C	C	L	C	C	5
#P535		X	B	B	L	B	B	B	5
#P722		X	B	B	B	L	B	B	5
#P809		X	—	B	B	B	L	B	4

C—Checker   B—Bagger   L—Lunch

---

[1] Edward Harwell, *Checkout Management.* (New York: Chain Store Publishing Corporation, 1963).

ANSWERS

12–1

(1) Straight $169.60
     Overtime $ 63.60
     Special $101.76
                $334.96

(2) Straight $234.00
     Overtime $124.80
     Special $187.20
                $546.00

(3) Straight $101.76
     Overtime $ 25.00
                $126.76

(4) Straight $150.00
     Overtime $ 56.30
                $206.30

(5) Straight $ 87.50
     Overtime $ 12.00
                $ 99.50

Work Space

Work Space

Work Space

Work Space

13

Operating Ratios

Food store managers, assistant managers, and department managers often are evaluated in terms of mathematical ratios which measure their effectiveness or ability. Obviously, any ratio or measure can be affected by outside factors which are beyond the control of the employee. Good management will be aware of this and should not hold an employee responsible for factors he cannot control. It is also obvious that an individual ratio may be out of line for a variety of good reasons (see below). Once again, good management should be aware of such differences.

However, under normal circumstances, the operating ratios discussed in this chapter can give a rough measure of an employee's performance. These ratios are quite important to the employee since his salary, promotion, and future may depend on them.

The normal operating ratios usually are based on gross sales volume in a given period—often a week.

It is important to realize at this point that, because of the rapid rate of inflation in recent years, many of our traditional measures have become antiquated. It would be most unfair to evaluate a store or employee on outdated ratios.

Many food retail people still quote ratios that are no longer valid, e.g. $7,000 per week per register. Such a figure is clearly outdated for two reasons: the dollar sales of retail food stores have increased as a normal function of growth, and inflation has pushed prices far above previous maximums. Operating ratios that were standard or stable for several years are now almost useless; most textbooks and guidebooks have not caught up to current levels.

Some of the more important ratios, with examples and problems, follow.

13-1 PRESENT SALES AS COMPARED WITH PAST SALES

A new manager in a store or a store with new equipment or new personnel often will be evaluated on this basis.

Examples:

1. A new store manager raises gross sales from $90,000 per week to $130,000 per week. What is the percentage increase?

First, subtract: $130,000 − $90,000 = $40,000 (the amount of increase or decrease)

Then, divide the increase or decrease by the original figure:

$$\frac{\$40,000}{\$90,000} = 44\% \text{ increase in sales.}$$

2. A frozen food department gets all new equipment, but sales decrease from $1,200 per week to $975 per week. Calculate effectiveness.

Subtract: $1,200 − $975 = $225

Then, divide the increase or decrease by the original figure:

$$\frac{\$225}{\$1,200} = 19\% \text{ decrease in sales.}$$

Problems 13–1

(1) Store sales increase from $108,000 per week to $124,000 per week. Calculate effectiveness.
(2) Store sales increase from $227,000 per week to $263,000 per week. Calculate effectiveness.
(3) Produce sales decrease from $18,000 per week to $16,250 per week. Calculate effectiveness.

13–2 SALES IN COMPARISON TO SIMILAR STORES

Many food chains divide their stores into categories or modules. Then the results of managers of similar stores are often compared against each other.

Example: Store A increases sales from $100,000 to $112,000 per week. A similar unit, Store B, increases sales from $102,000 to $115,000 per week. Which manager is more effective?

Store A $112,000 − $100,000 = $12,000

$$\frac{\$\ 12,000}{\$100,000} = 12\%$$

Store B $115,000 − $102,000 = $13,000

$$\frac{\$\ 13,000}{\$102,000} = 12.7\%$$

Store B has a slightly better sales increase.

Problems 13–2

(1) Store X increases sales from $88,000 per week to $96,000 per week. Store Y increases sales from $90,000 per week to $99,000 per week. Compare effectiveness.
(2) Store P has a sales decrease from $100,000 to $96,000 per week. Store Q has a sales decrease from $102,000 to $99,000. Compare effectiveness.

13-3 SALES IN COMPARISON TO COMPETITION

This often may be a very unfair comparison because many factors beyond the manager's control may change a competitor's sales, and hearsay is the usual source of competitions' figures. Nevertheless, this type of comparison is often used; the good manager knows he must live with it.

Example: Sales of Store X increase from $276,000 to $305,000 per week, while a similar competing store increases from $253,000 to $278,000. Compare effectiveness.

Store X $305,000 - $276,000 = $29,000

$$\frac{\$\ 29,000}{\$276,000} = 10.5\% \ \ \text{increase}$$

Competitor $278,000 - $253,000 = $25,000

$$\frac{\$\ 25,000}{\$253,000} = 9.9\% \ \ \text{increase}$$

Store X has a more significant increase.

There are two other important points worth mentioning. The store manager will not complain when he does better than his competitor because of external factors—only when he does worse. Moreover, a new or redesigned store usually will do better than average during the initial promotion period. Consumers' curiosity usually causes them to react favorably to a new or redecorated store. Obviously, neither a store nor a manager can be compared fairly with other stores or managers during such a period.

Problems 13-3

(1) Sales for Store Z decrease from $110,000 to $107,000 per week, while sales for a similar competitor decline from $108,000 to $104,000. Compare results.

(2) A close competitor increases sales from $180,000 to $190,000, while Store Y increases from $175,000 to $190,000. Compare results.

13–4 SALES PER SQUARE FOOT OR METER

Food stores come in many different sizes, and it is unfair to measure gross sales of a large store against those of a small or medium-size store. For this reason, there are a variety of operating ratios based on store size. Most companies have a group of comparison modules based on store size. Some of the more common ratios are:

- Sales per square foot or meter of total store space.
- Sales per square foot or meter of actual selling space. (This is an important measure of retailing effectiveness as it eliminates consideration of storage space and/or wasted space.)
- Sales per front foot or meter, running foot or meter, square foot or meter, or cubic foot or meter of shelf or display space.

Examples:

1. Store M is 18,000 square meters with 15,000 square meters of selling space. Gross sales $100,000 per week. Calculate ratios.

    $$\text{Sales per sq. meter} = \frac{\$100,000}{18,000 \text{ sq. meters}}$$
    $$= \$5.55 \text{ per sq. meter}$$

    Sales per sq. meter of selling space
    $$= \frac{\$100,000}{15,000 \text{ sq. meters}}$$
    $$= \$6.67 \text{ per sq. meter}$$

2. The produce department of a store has 4,000 square feet of display space and weekly sales of $12,000. Calculate ratio.

    $$\text{Sales per sq. foot} = \frac{\$12,000}{4,000 \text{ sq. ft.}}$$
    $$= \$3.00 \text{ per sq. ft.}$$

Problems 13–4

(1)   Store T has gross sales of $225,000 per week, and the frozen
      food department has sales of $10,000 per week. The store is
      60,000 square feet, with 52,000 square feet of selling space.
      The frozen food department has 1,800 square feet of display
      space. Calculate all appropriate ratios.

(2)   Store S has gross sales of $400,000 per week, with produce
      contributing $25,000. The store is 108,000 square feet with
      92,000 square feet of selling space. The produce section is
      4,500 square feet. Calculate all appropriate ratios.

13–5 SALES PER DEPARTMENT

This type of ratio helps top management, the store manager,
and the department heads evaluate what is happening in each
store area and calculate the contribution of each department to
total store results.

The results of each department can then be compared to other
company stores, to competing operations, or to regional and national averages. The national food trade associations, along with
trade journals such as *Progressive Grocer* and *Chain Store Age*
are the best sources of current information on average figures.
Chain Store Age reported the following national averages for
1973.[1]

Department	Average Margin	Share of Total Sales (%)	Gross Margin (%)
Fresh meat, fish, poultry	20.7	20.0	21.4
Produce	31.6	6.2	10.1
Frozen foods	22.2	4.9	5.7
Dairy & dairy products	18.2	12.7	11.8
Bakery & bakery products	16.9	10.9	10.9
Dry groceries	17.4	29.5	24.5
Non-foods & general merchandise	23.6	15.8	15.6
	19.4 (Store Average)	100.0	100.0

[1] "Performance in Supers by Department.' *Chain Store Age*, July, 1974
p. 65.

These results may vary depending on how many categories a store uses and what is included in each category. They also vary by geographic region, and they clearly change over periods of time as stores alter their product mix to conform to their customers' changing buying habits. However, such averages can be very helpful measures if used consistently.

Another major problem with departmental ratios is that the large increase in non-food products in supermarkets is pushing down the averages of the traditional food departments. The frozen food department is a good example. Frozen food experts were always predicting and hoping for a 10 percent share of store sales. However, with the rapid growth of non-food products in food stores, the frozen food industry has been forced to settle for a five percent share or less.

Example: Store A has sales of $312,000 per week with dry groceries totaling $120,000; produce, $30,000; and frozen food, $14,800. Calculate ratios.

Dry grocery contribution: $\dfrac{\$120,000}{\$312,000} = 38\%$

Produce contribution: $\dfrac{\$30,000}{\$312,000} = 10\%$

Frozen food contribution: $\dfrac{\$14,800}{\$312,000} = 5\%$

Problem 13–5

A store has gross sales of $200,000 per week and the departments contribute the following totals:

Meat, fish, and poultry	$40,000
Produce	$22,000
Frozen foods	$12,000
Dairy	$18,000
Bakery	$10,000
Dry groceries	$72,000
Non-foods	$26,000

Calculate all appropriate ratios.

13-6 SALES PER MAN-HOUR

This ratio is very important since it gives management a measure of employees' productivity, as well as measuring how well the manager is using his personnel.

Examples: 1.   Store D has sales of $200,000 per week and averages 2,000 man-hours. Calculate ratio of sales per man-hour.

$$\frac{\$200,000}{2,000} = \$100 \text{ per man-hour}$$

2.   Store E stacks 2,500 cases per week at an average of 1,000 man-hours. Calculate cases stacked per man-hour:

$$\frac{25,000}{1,000} = 25 \text{ cases per man-hour}$$

Problem 13-6

A store has gross sales of $300,000 per week, and uses 3,150 man-hours per week. Calculate the sales per man-hour ratio.

13-7 SALES PER REGISTER OR CHECKOUT

This ratio gives the manager a measure of how well he is using his checkouts or individual checkers. Once again, it should be warned that inflation has made many old "rule of thumb" measures obsolete.

Example: Store M has gross sales of $100,000 and 10 checkout registers. Calculate sales per checkout.

$$\frac{\$100,000}{10 \text{ registers}} = \$10,000 \text{ per register}$$

Problem 13-7

A store has sales of $180,000 per week and is using 12 checkouts. Calculate sales per register.

13-8 CONCLUSION

These last problems are designed to compare many of the factors discussed in this chapter.

Problems 13-8

(1)   There are two supermarkets in direct competition. Store A has gross sales of $200,000 per week with 20,000 square meters of space, 10 checkouts, and 2,000 man-hours. Store B has $180,000 gross sales, 18,000 square meters, 12 checkouts, and 2,000 man-hours. If all other factors are equal, which manager is doing the better job?

(2)   Store C is converting to the metric system. It has 100,000 square feet, with 91,000 square feet of selling space. Meat has 20,000 square feet, with 8,000 square feet for produce. The normal temperature is 68°F. Make the proper conversions of these figures to the metric system.

(3)   Compare Stores Y and Z:

	STORE Y	STORE Z
Gross Sales	$400,000	$396,000
Store Size	108,000 sq. ft.	110,000 sq. ft.
Checkouts	20	18
Man-Hours	4,000	3,600

ANSWERS

13–1

(1) $124,000 - $108,000 = $16,000

$$\frac{\$16,000}{\$108,000} = 15\% \text{ increase}$$

(2) $263,000 - $227,000 = $36,000

$$\frac{\$36,000}{\$227,000} = 16\% \text{ increase}$$

(3) $18,000 - $16,250 = $1,750

$$\frac{\$1,750}{\$18,000} = 10\% \text{ decrease}$$

13–2

(1) $96,000 - $88,000 = $8,000 $\dfrac{\$8,000}{\$88,000} = 9\%$ Store X

$99,000 - $90,000 = $9,000 $\dfrac{\$9,000}{\$90,000} = 10\%$ Store Y

Store Y had the greater increase.

(2) $100,000 - $96,000 = $4,000 $\dfrac{\$4,000}{\$100,000} = 4\%$ Store P

$102,000 - $99,000 = $3,000 $\dfrac{\$3,000}{\$102,000} = 3\%$ Store Q

Store Q had a smaller decrease.

13–3

(1) $110,000 - $107,000 = $3,000 $\dfrac{\$3,000}{\$110,000} = 2.7\%$

$108,000 - $104,000 = $4,000 $\dfrac{\$4,000}{\$108,000} = 3.7\%$

Competitor has greater decrease.

(2) $190,000 - $180,000 = $10,000 $\dfrac{\$10,000}{\$180,000} = 5.5\%$

$190,000 - $175,000 = $15,000 $\dfrac{\$15,000}{\$175,000} = 8.6\%$

Store Y has the greater increase.

13–4

(1) 1. $\dfrac{\$225,000}{60,000 \text{ sq. ft.}} = \$3.75 \text{ per sq. ft.}$

2. $\dfrac{\$225,000}{52,000 \text{ sq. ft.}} = \$4.33 \text{ per square foot of selling space}$

3. $\dfrac{\$10,000}{1,800 \text{ sq. ft.}} = \$5.55 \text{ per square foot of display space}$

(2) 1. $\dfrac{\$400,000}{108,000 \text{ sq. ft.}} = \$3.70 \text{ per sq. ft.}$

2. $\dfrac{\$400,000}{92,000 \text{ sq. ft.}} = \$4.35 \text{ per square foot of selling space}$

3. $\dfrac{\$25,000}{4,500 \text{ sq.ft.}} = \$5.55 \text{ per square foot of space}$

13–5

Meat $\dfrac{\$40,000}{\$200,000} = 20\%$ Bakery $\dfrac{\$10,000}{\$200,000} = 5\%$

Produce $\dfrac{\$22,000}{\$200,000} = 11\%$ Dry groceries $\dfrac{\$72,000}{\$200,000} = 36\%$

Frozen $\dfrac{\$12,000}{\$200,000} = 6\%$ Non-foods $\dfrac{\$26,000}{\$200,000} = 13\%$

Dairy $\dfrac{\$18,000}{\$200,000} = 9\%$ $\overline{100\%}$

13–6

$\dfrac{\$300,000}{3,150 \text{ man-hours}} = \$95 \text{ per man-hour}$

13–7

$\dfrac{\$180,000}{12} = \$15,000 \text{ per register}$

13–8

(1) **Store A**

$$\frac{\$200,000}{20,000 \text{ sq. meters}} = \$10 \text{ per sq. meter}$$

$$\frac{\$200,000}{10 \text{ registers}} = \$20,000 \text{ per register}$$

$$\frac{\$200,000}{2,000 \text{ man-hours}} = \$100 \text{ per man-hour}$$

Store B

$$\frac{\$180,000}{18,000 \text{ sq. meters}} = \$10 \text{ per sq. meter}$$

$$\frac{\$180,000}{12 \text{ registers}} = \$15,000 \text{ per register}$$

$$\frac{\$180,000}{2,000 \text{ man-hours}} = \$90 \text{ per man-hour}$$

Store A is making more effective use of checkouts and personnel than Store B.

(2) Store: 9,000 m²   Selling space: 8,280 m²
     Meat: 1,800 m²   Temperature: 20°C.
     Produce: 720 m²

(3) **Store Y**

$$\frac{\$400,000}{108,000 \text{ sq. ft.}} = \$3.70 \text{ per sq. ft.}$$

$$\frac{\$400,000}{20 \text{ registers}} = \$20,000 \text{ per register}$$

$$\frac{\$400,000}{4,000 \text{ man-hours}} = \$100 \text{ per man-hour}$$

Store Z

$$\frac{\$396,000}{110,000 \text{ sq. ft.}} = \$3.60 \text{ per sq. ft.}$$

$$\frac{\$396,000}{18 \text{ registers}} = \$22,000 \text{ per register}$$

$$\frac{\$396,000}{3,600 \text{ man-hours}} = \$110 \text{ per man-hour}$$

Store Z is doing a more effective job than Store Y.

Work Space

Work Space

Work Space

Work Space

14

Retail Food Store Operating Problems

This final chapter attempts to tie together all of the ideas, examples, and problems discussed in the earlier chapters. Each problem or case is fairly long and contains many separate problems that illustrate the varied situations involving mathematical computations facing the food store employee.

14–1

Super-Duper Markets is converting one of its stores to the metric system. This is being done as a public service gesture to aid their customers in understanding the new system. Make the necessary conversions.

	Present System	**Metric System**
(1)	Store, 20,000 sq. ft.	
(2)	Measurements, 200 feet long x 100 feet wide	
(3)	Selling Space, 18,000 square feet	
(4)	Meat Department, 4,000 square feet	

Present System	**Metric System**

(5)   Frozen Food Display Space, 80 linear feet
(6)   Frozen Turkeys average 18 pounds
(7)   Steaks average 2.5 pounds
(8)   Watermelons average 3 pounds
(9)   Canned Soup averages 10.5 ounces
(10) Frozen Peas average 6.5 ounces
(11) Apples average 3 pound bag
(12) Frozen Food stored at 20° F.
(13) Store Temperature is 68° F.

14–2

(1)   The meat manager wishes to maintain a 3 to 1 ratio for chicken breasts versus legs. If he has 300 legs, how many breasts does he need?

(2)   If a store has sales of $8,000 per week, with a net profit of $600, what sales are needed to net $800?

14–3

Calculate a simple operating statement for Store B. Gross sales are $600,000, cost of goods sold are $500,000, expenses are $88,000.

14–4

Store X wishes to raise the margin on all frozen foods to 22 percent. Calculate the new selling price.

(1)   Peas cost $.29
(2)   Apple pie costs $.89
(3)   Eclairs cost $1.19
(4)   Corn on the cob costs $.69
(5)   Orange juice costs $.08
(6)   Turkey costs $.42 a pound
(7)   Pizza costs $.33
(8)   Strawberries cost $.18
(9)   Soup costs $.12
(10) Topping costs $.94

14–5

Store Z has an average inventory of $90,000. Calculate the monthly turnover.

Monthly Sales

(1)	January	$180,000	(7)	July	$190,000
(2)	February	$160,000	(8)	August	$188,000
(3)	March	$182,000	(9)	September	$190,000
(4)	April	$185,000	(10)	October	$215,000
(5)	May	$200,000	(11)	November	$235,000
(6)	June	$210,000	(12)	December	$250,000

14–6

Discount the following items by 6% :

(1)	Peas	$ .19	(6)	Eggs	$ .99
(2)	Corn	$ .21	(7)	Butter	$1.04
(3)	Apples	$ .89	(8)	Sugar	$2.15
(4)	Steak	$2.39	(9)	Anti-freeze	$4.98
(5)	Coffee	$1.09	(10)	Card table	$12.98

14–7

Calculate a store's payroll: Clerks, $3.35 per hour; butchers, $4.80 per hour; department heads, $5.10 per hour. Do each individual's wages:

(1)	Clerk	12 hours	(6)	Clerk	60 hours
(2)	Clerk	40 hours	(7)	Butcher	40 hours
(3)	Clerk	50 hours	(8)	Butcher	42 hours
(4)	Clerk	32 hours	(9)	Grocery Manager	60 hours
(5)	Clerk	18 hours	(10)	Produce Manager	40 hours

14–8

The following are the operating data for one week at Save-Money Store B. Calculate the appropriate measures.

Sales, $375,000; beginning inventory, $15,000; ending inventory, $18,000; purchases, $290,000.

Expenses

Depreciation	$2,900	Advertising	$ 2,700
Insurance	$1,800	Salaries	$24,000
Linen	$ 600	Social security	$ 800
Heat-light	$5,400	Supplies	$ 4,500
Rent	$4,200	Taxes	$ 1,500
Repairs	$1,825	Delivery	$ 1,000
		Other	$18,000

14–9

The following are the margins per department and percentage share of sales for Wonder Mart Store D. Evaluate the margin found and calculate the appropriate sales percentages.

Department	Margin	Sales
Meat	18.2%	$ 200,000
Produce	30.0%	$ 70,000
Frozen food	23.2%	$ 38,000
Dairy	17.9%	$ 120,500
Bakery	16.3%	$ 100,000
Groceries	20.1%	$ 300,000
Non-food	24.0%	$ 180,000
	20.0% (Store Average)	$1,008,500

14–10

Food, Inc. presents the following figures for a new store in Marlboro Township:

Sales, $900,000; cost of goods sold, $725,000; advertising, $20,000; labor, $100,000; rent, $30,000; other expenses, $12,000

Calculate the proper measures.

14–11

The following are the operating data for Store H in Stonehope County.

Gross sales, $425,000; cost of goods sold, $340,000; salaries, $45,000; rent, $18,000; promotions, $36,000; other expenses, $14,000.

Calculate the appropriate measures.

14–12

Marvo Markets:

Gross sales, $198,000; cost of goods sold, $152,000;

expenses:

Salary	$23,500
Maintenance	$ 400
Supplies	$ 980
Heat, light, power	$ 3,300
Promotion	$ 250
Interest	$ 425
Security	$ 200
Taxes	$ 1,000
Rent	$ 7,600
Insurance	$ 410
Depreciation	$ 970
Other	$ 8,000

Calculate the appropriate measures.

14–13

Big Daddy Markets:

Gross sales, $500,000; cost of goods sold, $402,000;

expenses:

Advertising	$ 4,800
Amortization	$ 100

Depreciation	$ 4,500
Administration	$ 2,500
Insurance	$ 1,600
Interest	$ 2,850
Legal	$ 150
Linen	$ 400
Heat, light, power	$ 2,500
Office	$ 300
Rent	$ 7,200
Repairs	$ 360
Salary	$40,000
Social security	$ 2,000
Supplies	$ 5,200
Taxes	$ 800
Telephone	$ 650
Travel	$ 500
Unemployment	$ 720

Calculate the proper measures.

14–14

A.B.C. Markets, Inc. is a small supermarket chain operating six stores in the Middle Atlantic states. The chain recently opened a new store, and the following data describe the operation.

The new store is 30,000 square feet, with 27,500 square feet of selling space. Grocery covers 16,000 square feet, with 3,000 square feet for meat, and 1,200 square feet for produce. The store has nine checkouts and uses 1,200 man-hours per week. Sales have averaged $108,000 per week for the first quarter, with meat sales at $24,000, produce sales at $7,000, and grocery sales at $33,000. The average inventory is $56,000. A.B.C. reported for the first quarter gross sales of $1,404,000 with a cost of goods sold of $1,123,000. Labor expense was $126,000 and other expenses, $112,000.

Calculate the appropriate ratios and measures to evaluate the performance of the new store. Use the ratios discussed earlier in the book or add any you feel are relevant.

14–15

X.Y.Z. Markets, Inc. is a small supermarket chain operating six stores in the Southwest. It has just opened a new store, and it reports the following information.

The store is 25,000 square feet, with 21,000 square feet of selling space. The departments are as follows:

Grocery	13,000 square feet
Meat	2,800 square feet
Produce	1,000 square feet

The store has seven checkouts and uses 900 man-hours per week. Sales averaged $88,000 per week for the first quarter with the following breakdown:

Meat	$16,000
Produce	$ 7,000
Grocery	$27,000
Average Inventory	$46,000

The first quarter statement showed gross sales of $1,144,000, with cost of goods sold at $938,000. Labor expenses were $91,500 and other expenses were $90,000.

Calculate the appropriate ratios.

14–16

Compare and contrast the various operating efficiencies of A.B.C. Markets versus X.Y.Z. Markets.

ANSWERS

14–1

Metric System

(1)	18,000 m²	(8)	1.35 kg
(2)	6,000 cm×3,000 cm	(9)	29.7 g
(3)	16,200 m²	(10)	18.2 g
(4)	3,600 m²	(11)	1.35 kg
(5)	2,400 cm	(12)	−6.7°C
(6)	8.1 kg	(13)	20°C
(7)	1.13 kg		

14–2

(1)   900 chicken breasts
(2) $10,667

14–3

		Percentages
Gross Sales	$600,000	100%
− Cost of Goods Sold	$500,000	83%
Gross Margin	$100,000	17%
− Expenses	$ 88,000	15%
Net Profit	$ 12,000	2%

14–4

(1)	$ .37	(6)	$ .54
(2)	$1.14	(7)	$ .42
(3)	$1.53	(8)	$ .23
(4)	$ .88	(9)	$ .15
(5)	$ .10	(10)	$1.21

14–5

(1)	2.0	(7)	2.11
(2)	1.78	(8)	2.09
(3)	2.02	(9)	2.11
(4)	2.05	(10)	2.39
(5)	2.22	(11)	2.61
(6)	2.33	(12)	2.78

14–6

(1)	$ .18	(6)	$ .93
(2)	$ .20	(7)	$ .98
(3)	$ .84	(8)	$ 2.02
(4)	$2.25	(9)	$ 4.68
(5)	$1.02	(10)	$12.20

14–7

(1)	$ 40.20	(6)	$201.00
(2)	$134.00	(7)	$192.00
(3)	$167.50	(8)	$201.60
(4)	$107.20	(9)	$306.00
(5)	$ 60.30	(10)	$204.00

14–8

Typical Statement

	$	%
Gross Sales	$375,000	100.0%
Beginning Inventory	$ 15,000	
Purchases	$290,000	
	$305,000	
− Ending Inventory	$ 18,000	
Cost of Goods Sold	$287,000	76.5%
Gross Profit	$ 88,000	23.5%

Expenses:

Advertising	$ 2,700	.7%
Depreciation	$ 2,900	.8%
Insurance	$ 1,800	.5%
Linen	$ 600	.2%
Heat-light	$ 5,400	1.4%
Rent	$ 4,200	1.1%
Repairs	$ 1,825	.5%
Salary	$24,000	6.4%
Social security	$ 800	.2%
Supplies	$ 4,500	1.2%
Taxes	$ 1,500	.4%
Delivery	$ 1,000	.3%
Other expenses	$18,000	4.8%
− Total Expenses		$ 69,225	18.5%
Net Profit		$ 18,775	5.0%

Net profit at 5.2 percent is very good. The major reason appears to be the low payroll expense at 6.4 percent. This is probably a non-union store with a fairly low wage rate.

14–9

Margins

The 20 percent store margin is a good average. However, there are a few internal problems. The meat margin is low, 18.2 percent, and is being supported by a high grocery margin, 20.1 percent.

It would appear that either of two factors are at work. The store is in a highly competitive meat market, or it is using meat as a price leader in advertising. This may be dangerous since grocery prices are probably higher than they should be.

Sales

	%
Meat	19.8
Produce	6.8
Frozen food	3.8
Dairy	12.0
Bakery	10.0
Grocery	29.8
Non-food	17.8
	100.0%

This is a fairly normal distribution. The frozen food figure is quite low, 3.8 percent; however, the non-food figure, 17.8 percent, is high enough to offset the difference.

14–10

	$	$	%
Gross Sales		$900,000	100.0%
−Cost of Goods Sold		$725,000	80.6%
Gross Profit		$175,000	19.4%
Expenses			
Advertising	$ 20,000		2.2%
Labor	$100,000		11.2%
Rent	$ 30,000		3.3%
Other	$ 12,000		1.3%
Total Expense	$162,000		18.0%
−Total Expense		$162,000	18.0%
Net Profit		$ 13,000	1.4%

The net profit figure of 1.4 percent is somewhat low, and is probably caused by the high labor cost of 11.2 percent.

14–11

	$	%
Gross Sales	$425,000	100.0%
−Cost of Goods Sold	$340,000	80.0%
Gross Profit	$ 85,000	20.0%

Expenses

Salary	$45,000	10.6%
Rent	$18,000	4.2%
Promotions	$36,000	8.5%
Other	$14,000	3.3%
−Total Expense	$113,000	26.6%
Net Profit (Loss)	−$28,000	−6.6%

Here we see a store with a net loss of $28,000. The loss is directly traceable to the high promotion budget of 8.5 percent. This must be a new store, and perhaps it is the first time this company has operated in this particular market area. The company is spending very heavily on promotion in order to gain entry into the market.

This store should do better after this initial period, since the other figures are quite normal.

14–12

	$	%
Gross Sales	$198,000	100.0%
−Cost of Goods Sold	$152,000	76.8%
Gross Profit	$ 46,000	23.2%
Expenses:		
Salary	$23,500	11.9%
Maintenance	$ 400	.2%
Supplies	$ 980	.5%
Heat, light, power	$ 3,300	1.7%
Promotion	$ 250	.1%
Interest	$ 425	.2%
Security	$ 200	.1%
Taxes	$ 1,000	.5%
Rent	$ 7,600	3.8%
Insurance	$ 410	.2%
Depreciation	$ 970	.5%
Others	$ 8,000	4.0%
−Total Expenses	$ 47,035	23.7%
Net Profit (Loss)	−$ 1,035	−0.5%

Here again we have a net loss, of .5 percent. The loss is small, but it is nevertheless disturbing because the store has good data with the exception of the high (four percent) and unexplained "other expense" figure.

This could be the result of poor accounting control, or because the owners are hiding some unusual expenses in this store. If the latter is the case, it is, of course, most unfair to the manager.

14–13

		$	%
Gross Sales		$500,000	100.0%
−Cost of Goods Sold		$402,000	80.4%
Gross Profit		$ 98,000	19.6%
Expenses:			
Advertising	$ 4,800		1.0%
Amortization	$ 100		—
Depreciation	$ 4,500		.9%
Administration	$ 2,500		.5%
Insurance	$ 1,600		.3%
Interest	$ 2,850		.6%
Legal	$ 150		—
Heat, light, power	$ 2,500		.5%
Linen	$ 400		—
Office	$ 300		—
Rent	$ 7,200		1.4%
Repairs	$ 360		—
Salary	$40,000		8.0%
Social security	$ 2,000		.4%
Supplies	$ 5,200		1.0%
Taxes	$ 800		.2%
Telephone	$ 650		.1%
Travel	$ 500		.1%
Unemployment	$ 720		.1%
−Total Expenses		$ 77,130	15.4%
Net Profit		$ 20,870	4.2%

This is a good example of a store with a fairly normal operating statement.

14–14

(1) Sales per square foot, $3.60
(2) Sales per square foot of selling space, $3.93
(3) Grocery sales per square foot, $2.06
(4) Meat sales per square foot, $8.00
(5) Produce sales per square foot, $5.83
(6) Sales per checkout, $12,000
(7) Sales per man-hour, $90
(8) Turnover, 1.93
(9) Operating Statement:

A.B.C. Market

		$	%
Gross Sales		$1,404,000	100.0%
−Cost of Goods Sold		−$1,123,000	80.0%
Gross Margin		$ 281,000	20.0%
−Labor	$126,000		9.0%
−Expense	$112,000		8.0%
Total Expense		−$ 238,000	17.0%
Net Profit		$ 43,000	3.0%

14–15

(1) Sales per square foot, $3.52
(2) Sales per square foot of selling space, $4.19
(3) Grocery sales per square foot, $2.08
(4) Meat sales per square foot, $5.71
(5) Produce sales per square foot, $7.00
(6) Sales per checkout, $12,571
(7) Sales per man-hour, $98
(8) Turnover, 1.91
(9) Operating Statement:

X.Y.Z. Market

	$		%
Gross Sales	$1,155,000		100.0%
−Cost of Goods Sold	−$ 938,000		81.2%
Gross Margin	$ 217,000		18.8%
−Labor Expenses $91,500		8.0%	
−Expenses $90,000		7.8%	
Total Expense	−$ 181,500		15.8%
Net Profit	$ 35,500		3.0%

14–16

(1) Sales per square foot: almost the same.

(2) Sales per square foot of selling space: this can be deceiving. A.B.C. uses 91 percent of its space for selling versus only 84 percent for X.Y.Z., so the higher ratio for X.Y.Z. is misleading.

(3) Grocery per square foot: almost the same.

(4) Meat per square foot: A.B.C. better, possibly because of the Middle Atlantic location.

(5) Produce per square foot: X.Y.Z. better, possibly because of the Southwest location.

(6) Sales per checkout: slight advantage to X.Y.Z.

(7) Sales per man-hour: X.Y.Z. better.

(8) Turnover: almost the same.

(9) Operating Statement: A.B.C. has the better net profit despite higher labor costs. The reason is the cost of goods sold difference (two percent).

(10) Overall: A.B.C. perhaps slightly more efficient, especially in purchasing of product mix.

Work Space

Work Space

Work Space

Work Space

Appendix

METRIC CONVERSION TABLES

Conversions To Metric Measures＊

Symbol	When You Know	Multiply by	To Find	Symbol
		LENGTH		
in.	inches	2.5	centimeters	cm
ft.	feet	30	centimeters	cm
yd.	yards	0.9	meters	m
mi.	miles	1.6	kilometers	km
		AREA		
in.^{2}	sq. inches	6.5	sq. centimeters	cm^2
ft.^{2}	sq. feet	0.09	sq. meters	m^2
yd.^{2}	sq. yards	0.8	sq. meters	m^2
mi.^{2}	sq. miles	2.6	sq. kilometers	km^2
	acres	0.4	hectares	ha

Symbol	When You Know	Multiply by	To Find	Symbol
MASS (weight)				
oz.	ounces	28	grams	g
lb.	pounds	0.45	kilograms	kg
	short tons (2,000 lb)	0.9	tonnes	t
VOLUME				
tsp.	teaspoons	5	millileters	ml
Tbsp.	tablespoons	15	milliliters	ml
fl. oz.	fluid ounces	30	milliliters	ml
c.	cups	0.24	liters	l
pt.	pints	0.47	liters	l
qt.	quarts	0.95	liters	l
gal.	gallons	3.8	liters	l
ft.^{3}	cubic feet	0.03	cubic meters	m^3
yd.^{3}	cubic yards	0.76	cubic meters	m^3
TEMPERATURE (exact)				
°F	Fahrenheit temperature	$\frac{5}{9}$ (after substracting 32)	Celsius temperature	°C

* Source: U.S. Department of Commerce.

Conversions From Metric Measures*

Symbol	When You Know	Multiply by	To Find	Symbol
LENGTH				
mm	millimeters	0.04	inches	in.
cm	centimeters	0.4	inches	in.
m	meters	3.3	feet	ft.
m	meters	1.1	yards	yd.
km	kilometers	0.6	miles	mi.
AREA				
cm^2	sq. centimeters	0.16	sq. inches	in.^{2}
m^2	sq. meters	1.2	sq. yards	yd.^{2}
km^2	sq. kilometers	0.4	sq. miles	mi.^{2}
ha	hectares (10,000 kg)	2.5	acres	

Symbol	When You Know	Multiply by	To Find	Symbol
		MASS (weight)		
g	grams	0.035	ounces	oz.
kg	kilograms	2.2	pounds	lb.
t	tonnes (1,000 kg)	1.1	short tons	
		VOLUME		
ml	millileters	0.03	fluid ounces	fl. oz.
l	liters	2.1	pints	pt.
l	liters	1.06	quarts	qt.
l	liters	0.26	gallons	gal.
m^3	cubic meters	35	cubic feet	ft.^{3}
m^3	cubic meters	1.3	cubic yards	yd.^{3}
		TEMPERATURE (exact)		
°C	Celsius temperature	$\frac{9}{5}$ (then add 32)	Fahrenheit temperature	°F

* Source: U.S. Department of Commerce.

GROSS MARGIN AND MARKUP CONVERSION TABLE

Gross Margin Percentage of Selling Price	Markup Percentage of Cost
5.0	5.3
6.0	6.4
7.0	7.5
8.0	8.7
9.0	10.0
10.0	11.1
11.0	12.4
12.0	13.6
13.0	15.0
14.0	16.3
15.0	17.7
16.0	19.1
17.0	20.5
18.0	22.0
19.0	23.5
20.0	25.0
21.0	26.6
22.0	28.2

Gross Margin Percentage of Selling Price	Markup Percentage of Cost
23.0	29.9
24.0	31.6
25.0	33.3
26.0	35.0
27.0	37.0
28.0	39.0
29.0	40.9
30.0	42.9
31.0	45.0
32.0	47.1
33.0	49.3
34.0	51.5
35.0	53.9
36.0	56.3
37.0	58.8
38.0	61.3
39.0	64.0
40.0	66.7
41.0	70.0
42.0	72.4
43.0	75.4
44.0	78.6
45.0	81.8
46.0	85.2
47.0	88.7
48.0	92.3
49.0	96.1
50.0	100.0

Source: Leed/German, *Food Merchandising*, Chain Store Age Books, New York, 1973, p. 110.

CONVERSION FROM FRACTIONS TO DECIMALS

$$\frac{1}{64} = .016 \qquad \frac{3}{16} = .1875$$
$$\frac{1}{32} = .031 \qquad \frac{7}{32} = .219$$
$$\frac{1}{16} = 0.625 \qquad \frac{1}{4} = .25$$
$$\frac{3}{32} = .094 \qquad \frac{9}{32} = .281$$
$$\frac{1}{8} = .125 \qquad \frac{5}{16} = .3125$$
$$\frac{5}{32} = .156 \qquad \frac{11}{32} = .344$$

$$\frac{3}{8} = .375 \qquad \frac{23}{32} = .719$$
$$\frac{13}{32} = .406 \qquad \frac{3}{4} = .75$$
$$\frac{7}{16} = .4375 \qquad \frac{25}{32} = .781$$
$$\frac{15}{32} = .469 \qquad \frac{13}{16} = .8125$$
$$\frac{1}{2} = .50 \qquad \frac{27}{32} = .844$$
$$\frac{17}{32} = .531 \qquad \frac{7}{8} = .875$$
$$\frac{9}{16} = .563 \qquad \frac{29}{32} = .906$$
$$\frac{19}{32} = .594 \qquad \frac{15}{16} = .9375$$
$$\frac{5}{8} = .625 \qquad \frac{31}{32} = .969$$
$$\frac{21}{32} = .656 \qquad \frac{8}{8} = 1.00$$
$$\frac{11}{16} = .6875$$

TYPICAL SALES TAX TABLE

6% Sales Tax

Amount of Sale	Tax	Amount of Sale	Tax
$0.00 – $0.10	None	3.85 – 4.10	.24
.11 – .17	1¢	4.11 – 4.17	.25
.18 – .34	2¢	4.18 – 4.34	.26
.35 – .50	3¢	4.35 – 4.50	.27
.51 – .67	4¢	4.51 – 4.67	.28
.68 – .84	5¢	4.68 – 4.84	.29
.85 – 1.10	6¢	4.85 – 5.10	.30
1.11 – 1.17	7¢	5.11 – 5.17	.31
1.18 – 1.34	8¢	5.18 – 5.34	.32
1.35 – 1.50	9¢	5.35 – 5.50	.33
1.51 – 1.67	$.10	5.51 – 5.67	.34
1.68 – 1.84	.11	5.68 – 5.84	.35
1.85 – 2.10	.12	5.85 – 6.10	.36
2.11 – 2.17	.13	6.11 – 6.17	.37
2.18 – 2.34	.14	6.18 – 6.34	.38
2.35 – 2.50	.15	6.35 – 6.50	.39
2.51 – 2.67	.16	6.51 – 6.67	.40
2.68 – 2.84	.17	6.68 – 6.84	.41
2.85 – 3.10	.18	6.85 – 7.10	.42
3.11 – 3.17	.19	7.11 – 7.17	.43
3.18 – 3.34	.20	7.18 – 7.34	.44
3.35 – 3.50	.21	7.35 – 7.50	.45
3.51 – 3.67	.22	7.51 – 7.67	.46
3.68 – 3.84	.23	7.68 – 7.84	.47

Amount of Sale	Tax	Amount of Sale	Tax
7.85 – 8.10	.48	9.35 – 9.50	.57
8.11 – 8.17	.49	9.51 – 9.67	.58
8.18 – 8.34	.50	9.68 – 9.84	.59
8.35 – 8.50	.51	9.85 – 10.10	.60
8.51 – 8.67	.52	Over–$10.00	.60+
8.68 – 8.84	.53	Over–$20.00	1.20+
8.85 – 9.10	.54	Over–$30.00	1.80+
9.11 – 9.17	.55	Over–$40.00	2.40+
9.18 – 9.34	.56	Over–$50.00	3.00+

STANDARD WEIGHTS AND MEASURES

Troy Weight

24 grains	=	1 pwt.
20 pwts.		1 ounce
12 ounces		1 pound

Used for weighing gold, silver and jewels.

Apothecaries' Weight

20 grains	=	1 scruple
3 scruples		1 dram
8 drams		1 ounce
12 ounces		1 pound

The ounce and pound in this are the same as in Troy Weight.

Avoirdupois Weight

$27\frac{11}{32}$ grains =		1 dram
16 drams		1 ounce
16 ounces		1 pound
25 pounds		1 quarter
4 quarters		1 cwt.
2,000 lbs.		1 short ton
2,240 lbs.		1 long ton

Dry Measure

2 pints	=	1 quart
8 quarts		1 peck
4 pecks		1 bushel
36 bushels		1 chaldron

Liquid Measure

4 gills	=	1 pint
2 pints		1 quart
4 quarts		1 gallon
$31\frac{1}{2}$ gals.		1 barrel

Long Measure

12 inches	=	1 foot
3 feet		1 yard
$5\frac{1}{2}$ yds.		1 rod
40 rods		1 furlong
8 furlongs		1 sta. mile
3 miles		1 league

Cloth Measure

2¼ inches	=	1 nail
4 nails		1 quarter
4 quarters		1 yard

Surveyor's Measure

7.92 inches	=	1 link
25 links		1 rod
10 square chains or		
160 sq. rods		1 acre
640 acres		1 sq. mile
36 sq. miles or		
6 miles sq.		1 township
4 rods		1 chain

Square Measure

144 sq. inches	=	1 sq. ft.
9 sq. ft.		1 sq. yard
30¼ sq. yds.		1 sq. rod
40 sq. rods		1 rood
4 roods		1 acre
640 acres		1 sq. mile

Cubic Measure

1,728 cu. in.	=	1 cu. foot
128 cu. ft.		1 cord wood
27 cu. ft.		1 cu. yard
40 cu. ft.		1 ton shpg.
2,150.42 cu. in.		1 standard bushel
231 cu. in.		1 standard gal. liquid
1 cu. ft.		about ⅕ of a bushel
1 Perch		A mass 16½ ft. long, 1 ft. high and 1½ ft. wide, containing 24¾ cubic feet

Glossary

Addition	The process of combining two or more numbers to obtain a single quantity or result.
Advertising Allowance	An extra discount given by a manufacturer to a retailer if he uses the money to promote the manufacturer's product. Often referred to as cooperative advertising or "push money."
Average Inventory	The amount of stock normally needed to fill a particular section.
Blue Laws	A commonly used term that refers to old or religiously oriented laws that restrict all or certain types of commerce or restrict commerce on certain days or during certain hours.
Cash Discount	A small discount granted by a seller in order to encourage prompt payment by the buyer.
Convenience Store	A small retail food store that is typified by long hours, a convenient location, small product sizes, limited variety, national

brands, considerable non-food merchandise, and prices somewhat higher than those found in supermarkets.

Cost of Goods Sold The cost to the retailer for the merchandise in his store. Usually accounts for around 80 percent of gross sales.

Decimal System A system of notation which separates whole numbers and decimal fractions.

Division The process of finding how many times one number is combined in another.

Discount A markdown from some initial price usually for sale or promotional purposes.

Discounts Various types of price reductions offered by manufacturers to retailers.

Expenses The various costs incurred by retailers; often accounts for 20 percent of gross sales.

Fair Trade The practice whereby a manufacturer maintains a minimum price for his product at the retail level. Set by agreement, tradition, or law.

Federal Trade Commission A Federal agency which regulates false and misleading sales and advertising.

Food and Drug Administration A Federal agency which protects consumers from unsafe food and drug products through research and regulation of labels and additives.

Food Marketing All of the activities that take place in the distribution of food from farm to consumers' tables.

Food Stamps Discount coupons issued by the United States Department of Agriculture to low income families.

Fractions A part or portion of the totality of something.

Free Goods A method by which a manufacturer encourages a retailer to buy in large quantities, e.g., one free case given for every 10 purchased.

Functional Discount An extra price discount which goes to a retailer because he performs an extra marketing function, such as storage, transport, etc.

Gross Margin	The difference between a retailer's gross sales and his cost of goods sold.
Gross Sales	Total retail sales in a store, department, etc., for some given time period.
Inventory	The stock on hand in store, warehouse, department, etc.
Inventory Control	The practice of handling inventory to achieve its most profitable use.
List Price	The retail price of a product.
Margin	The difference between the retail price and the cost of an item, usually expressed as a percentage of the retail price.
Markdown	The difference between the original selling price of an item and a new, lower, discounted price, usually expressed as a percentage of the original price.
Markup	The difference between the retail price and the cost of an item, usually expressed as a percentage of the cost.
Metric System	The International System of Units (SI). The commonly accepted system of measurement in the world.
Multiplication	The process of combining one number as many times as there are units in another number which results in a product.
National Brand	A brand sponsored and/or distributed by a manufacturing or processing firm and available for sale in most retail stores.
Net Profit	The so-called "bottom line"; the returns to the enterprise after all expenses are paid.
Non-Price Competition	A method of competition in which the major marketing emphasis is on non-price factors such as service, brands, stamps, premiums, and coupons.
Nutritional Labeling	The practice of placing detailed nutritional information on the labels of food products.
Open Dating	The practice of stamping product with an easy-to-read date which indicates optimum shelf-life.
Operating Ratios	The various measures used to evaluate the performance of a store, manager, etc.
OSHA	The Occupational Safety and Health Administration, a federal agency which pro-

tects employees from injury and improper working conditions.

Out-of-Stock   An item not available for sale, either because of improper stocking or ordering or an unusually successful sales promotion.

Price Competition   A type of sales approach that uses low prices to attract customers.

Price by Measure   A method by which the price is calculated in relation to some normally accepted quantity or measure in order to allow the consumer to make more meaningful price and quality comparisons.

Private Brand   A brand sponsored and/or distributed by one wholesale or retail company.

Quantity Discount   A sizeable discount granted to a retailer for buying in larger quantities; legal if the size of the discount is proportional to the larger purchase.

Raincheck   A ticket allowing the customer to buy at a sale price an item which is temporarily out of stock.

Pull Date   The date the manufacturer recommends his product be removed from the retail shelf.

Sales Tax   A state or city tax levied on retail sales by many states and municipalities.

Shrink   Merchandise missing as a result of breakage, spoilage, shoplifting, etc.

Stockturn   See Turnover.

Subtraction   The process of finding the difference between numbers.

Supermarket   A retail food store where at least the meat, produce, and grocery sections are self-service.

Turnover   The rate at which the average total inventory in a department or store is sold; also applies to the rate of sale of a particular product.

Unit Price   The practice of selling each item as an individual unit, rather than on a multiple-unit basis.

U.P.C.   The Universal Product Code, a system of identification of all food products accepted by all segments of the food industry.

U.S.D.A.   The United States Department of Agriculture, which grades and inspects food products and generally supervises their production on the farm and the marketing process in general.

The Author

Daniel J. McLaughlin, Jr. co-editor (with Charles Mallowe) of *Food Marketing and Distribution*, is Assistant Professor and Acting Chairman of the Academy of Food Marketing at St. Joseph's College in Philadelphia.

Mr. McLaughlin is also the author (with Donald Dixon) of *The Dilemma of Inner City Food Shopping* and has written a series of management guides for the Super Market Institute.

He holds degrees from St. Joseph's College and Temple University and has done doctoral work at Temple and New York University. Mr. McLaughlin has contributed articles to such periodicals as *Business and Society, Social Science Quarterly, The Journal of Marketing Research, Quick Frozen Foods*, and *The Journal of Small Business Management.*

In addition to teaching and writing, Mr. McLaughlin has conducted several research studies on food retailing in the inner-city and has lectured before such groups as the National Association of Retail Grocers, the Food Distribution Research Society, and the American Marketing Association.